American Revolution
Battles and Leaders

American Revolution

Battles and Leaders

AARON R. MURRAY, EDITOR

DK Publishing, Inc.

LONDON, NEW YORK, MUNICH,
MELBOURNE, AND DELHI

DK PUBLISHING, INC.
Senior Editor Beth Sutinis
Assistant Managing Art Editor Michelle Baxter
Associate Editor Elizabeth Hester
Creative Director Tina Vaughan
Jacket Art Director Dirk Kaufman
Publisher Chuck Lang
Production Manager Chris Avgherinos

MEDIA PROJECTS INC.
Executive Editor Carter Smith
Editor Aaron R. Murray
Contributing Writer Stuart Murray
Consultants René Chartrand, Don Troiani
Designer Laura Smyth, Smythtype
Production Editor James Burmester
Copy Editor Kristen Behrens

First American Edition, 2004
04 05 06 10 9 8 7 6 5 4 3 2 1

Published in the United States
by DK Publishing, Inc.
375 Hudson Street
New York, New York 10014

A catalog record for this book is available
from the Library of Congress.

ISBN 0-7894-9889-8 (PB)
ISBN 0-7894-9888-X (HC)

Reproduced by Colourscan, Singapore
Printed and bound in China by
South China Printing Co., Ltd.

Discover more at
www.dk.com

*Halftitle: George Washington at Mount Vernon,
Virginia. Title page: British retreat from Concord,
Massachusetts, April 1775.*

CONTENTS

A REBELLION IS BORN 6

War for Independence **8**
Chronology of War **10**
Battles Map 1775–1783 **12**

ROYAL HIGHLAND
EMIGRANT REGIMENTAL
BELT PIECE

1775: THE FIGHT FOR LIBERTY BEGINS *14*

Lexington and Concord *16*
Battle of Breed's Hill *18*
Siege of Boston *20*
Invasion of Quebec *24*

HESSIAN CAP OF
REGIMENT VON
KNYPHAUSEN

1776: INDEPENDENCE, RETREAT, AND RALLY *28*

Battle of Moore's Creek *30*
Siege of Charleston (1st) *32*
Battle of Long Island *34*
Battle of Valcour Island *36*
Fall of Fort Washington *37*
Battle of Trenton *38*

BRITISH OFFICER'S SWORD

1777: A YEAR OF GREAT BATTLES 40

Battle of Princeton 42

Saratoga Campaign 44

Battle of Oriskany 46

Battles of Saratoga 48

Battle of Brandywine 50

Battle of Germantown 52

1778: FRANCE RENEWS HOPE FOR THE PATRIOTS 54

Battle of Monmouth 56

Long Knives' Campaign 58

LEXINGTON MILITIAMAN'S
WAISTCOAT

1779–1780: THE WAR GOES SOUTH, LOST BATTLES 60

Battle of Stony Point 62

Bonhomme Richard fights
    HMS *Serapis* 63

Siege of Savannah 64

Siege of Charleston (2nd) 66

Battle of Camden 67

Battle of King's Mountain 68

1781: WASHINGTON CLOSES THE RING 70

Battle of The Cowpens 72

Lafayette's Virginia Campaign 74

Siege of Pensacola 76

Battle of Guilford Court House 78

Battle of Eutaw Springs 80

Siege of Yorktown 82

NORTH CAROLINA SOLDIER'S
PEWTER BUTTON

1782–1783: AN UNEASY TRUCE, A WELCOME PEACE 86

Last Sieges and Battles 88

Evacuation Day 90

More Soldiers and Politicians 92

Index 95

Acknowledgments 96

GRAND UNION FLAG

A REBELLION IS BORN

The Seven Years' War between Great Britain and France raged around the world from 1756–1763. In the American colonies, this bloody conflict was called the French and Indian War.

ROYAL COAT OF ARMS

In the end, Britain was victorious, and France gave up Canada. Peace and prosperity came to America, whose 13 original British colonies were stronger than ever.

The Seven Years' War had put Great Britain deep in debt. To help pay for the war, Parliament and King George III decided to tax Americans. After all, the colonies had benefited greatly from victory and were growing rich trading with the British Empire. Parliament placed taxes and fees on printed documents and publications and on imports such as sugar and tea. Americans objected because they did not have representatives in Parliament. They called it illegal "taxation without representation."

Angry colonists refused to buy British goods, and some attacked government officials. Boston was especially hostile to the government. In 1768, thousands of soldiers occupied Boston to punish the city for its resistance. These troops were commanded by General Thomas Gage, who tried to keep peace but was unsuccessful. A secret anti-British organization called the "Sons of Liberty" attracted many members around the colonies. Conflicts erupted between the "Sons" and soldiers. In 1770, soldiers fired on a mob in what became called the "Boston Massacre."

Late in 1773, Bostonians dumped British tea into the harbor rather than pay taxes on it. Now Parliament laid harsh regulations on Massachusetts and closed Boston's port. The city suffered from lack of trade and commerce. Other colonies sent money and food to help Boston's citizens, many of whom were hungry. In 1774, a "Continental Congress" of colonial delegates met in Philadelphia to decide on a course of action.

By now, the 13 colonies had a population of 2.7 million. The Northern Colonies were Massachusetts, Connecticut, Rhode Island, and New Hampshire. Boston was the major seaport. The Middle Colonies were New York, New Jersey, Pennsylvania, and Delaware, with two large cities: Philadelphia and New York. The Southern Colonies were Virginia, Maryland, North Carolina, South Carolina, and Georgia. Charleston and Savannah were the largest cities there.

The First Continental Congress, meeting in Philadelphia, pledged to stop importing British goods. The colonies united to resist government oppression. In the spring of 1775, resistance exploded into armed rebellion at Lexington and Concord, Massachusetts. Revolution had begun.

ROYAL SPLENDOR

King George III ignored the warnings of those who said Britain could not overcome American armed resistance. Instead, he went along with the aggressive colonial policies of his Tory ministers and advisers. This brought on the American Revolution.

BRAVE FELLOWS ALL

A fife shrills and drums beat as Patriot soldiers follow their commander into a hail of enemy bullets at the Battle of Brandywine, Pennsylvania.

WAR FOR INDEPENDENCE

As delegates to the Continental Congress in Philadelphia decided America's future, revolutionary conflict spread throughout the colonies.

King George III had well-trained, confident regiments, but the American colonials also knew how to fight. Thousands had military experience from the French and Indian War. Some of the best commanders in that war were Americans, such as rangers Robert Rogers, John Stark, and Israel Putnam. Virginia colonel George Washington was widely respected as an excellent field officer.

After the war, British generals Thomas Gage and Guy Carleton continued their military service in North America. Other king's officers, such as Richard Montgomery and Horatio Gates, retired and became colonists themselves. During the Revolution former comrades-in-arms took opposing sides.

GREAT SEAL OF THE
UNITED STATES

A FATEFUL MOMENT
The Second Continental Congress looks on as the drafting committee submits the Declaration of Independence to John Hancock, president of Congress. Committee members were (l–r) John Adams, Roger Sherman, Robert Livingston, Thomas Jefferson, and Benjamin Franklin.

In many ways, this was a civil war that bitterly divided American communities and even families. A third of the colonials, called Patriots, supported the Revolution. A third, the Loyalists, fought against it. Another third did not take sides.

On July 4, 1776, after more than a year of warfare, the Second Continental Congress adopted The Declaration of Independence. There was no turning back. The liberty of the new United States of America would be decided by the leaders, on both sides, who commanded the soldiers in battle.

SILVER INKSTAND USED TO SIGN DECLARATION

AUTHORIZING REVOLUTION
One by one, the congressional delegates of the 13 colonies signed their names to the Declaration of Independence. John Hancock was first, his signature the largest. If the Revolution failed, these men could be executed for treason.

EIGHT YEARS OF STRUGGLE

1775

APRIL Lexington and Concord

MAY Second Continental Congress convenes in Philadelphia; John Hancock is elected president of Congress • Capture of Fort Ticonderoga

JUNE Congress votes unanimously to make George Washington commander-in-chief of the new Continental Army • Battle of Breed's Hill • Siege of Boston begins

JULY George Washington takes command of the army camped outside of Boston • Congress sends King George III the Olive Branch Petition, hoping to avoid a war • Benjamin Franklin establishes the American Post Office, and is the first Postmaster General

AUGUST King George III refuses to receive the Olive Branch Petition and issues a Proclamation declaring the colonies in open rebellion

SEPTEMBER Richard Montgomery and Benedict Arnold begin invasions of Canada

NOVEMBER Congress establishes a Continental Navy

1776

WASHINGTON CROSSES THE DELAWARE

JANUARY "Common Sense" by Thomas Paine is published • Henry Knox brings Fort Ticonderoga's guns to Cambridge, Massachusetts

FEBRUARY Battle of Moore's Creek Bridge, North Carolina

MARCH British evacuate Boston

MAY France begins sending arms and ammunition to the colonies • Americans begin retreat from Canada

JUNE Siege of Charleston, South Carolina

JULY The Declaration of Independence is signed • Howe's fleet arrives in New York Harbor

AUGUST Battle of Long Island • Washington evacuates Brooklyn by night and saves his army

SEPTEMBER Battle of Harlem Heights • The Great Fire of New York destroys much of the city • Nathan Hale is executed for spying on the British in New York

OCTOBER Battle of Valcour Island • Washington is defeated at the Battle of White Plains, New York

NOVEMBER Fall of Fort Washington and Fort Lee on the Hudson River • Washington retreats through New Jersey

DECEMBER Battle of Trenton • Benjamin Franklin travels to France

1777

HERKIMER AT ORISKANY

JANUARY Battle of Princeton • Washington's army goes into winter quarters at Morristown, New Jersey

JUNE Congress mandates a flag of 13 stars and 13 stripes • British general John Burgoyne begins invasion south from Canada

JULY Burgoyne recaptures Fort Ticonderoga • Battle of Hubbardton, Vermont

AUGUST Battle of Oriskany • Battle of Bennington

SEPTEMBER Battle of Brandywine • Philadelphia falls to Howe • First Battle of Saratoga

OCTOBER Battle of Germantown • Burgoyne surrenders after Second Battle of Saratoga

NOVEMBER Congress adopts Articles of Confederation, basis of government for the United States of America

DECEMBER Washington's army goes into winter quarters at Valley Forge, Pennsylvania

1778

FEBRUARY France signs treaty of alliance with United States • Prussian Baron von Steuben arrives and begins training the Continental Army at Valley Forge

MAY General Henry Clinton replaces General William Howe as commander of British forces in America

JUNE Battle of Monmouth, New Jersey • Virginian George Rogers Clark begins his campaign

JULY Congress returns to Philadelphia • Loyalists and Indians massacre settlers in Wyoming Valley, Pennsylvania • France declares war on Britain

AUGUST French and Americans fail in their siege of British-held Newport, Rhode Island

1779

BONHOMME RICHARD DEFEATS HMS *SERAPIS*

JUNE Spain declares war on Britain

JULY Battle of Stony Point

SEPTEMBER Captain John Paul Jones's *Bonhomme Richard* sinks HMS *Serapis*

OCTOBER Siege of Savannah • Washington sets up winter quarters at Morristown for what will be another harsh winter

1780

MARCH Siege of Charleston begins

MAY In the greatest American defeat of the war, General Benjamin Lincoln surrenders Charleston to British commander Sir Henry Clinton

JUNE Horatio Gates is chosen by Congress to command the Southern Continental Army

JULY 5,000 French troops commanded by Count de Rochambeau arrive at Newport, Rhode Island

AUGUST Gates's army is destroyed by Cornwallis at Camden, North Carolina

SEPTEMBER American General Benedict Arnold goes over to the British.

OCTOBER Battle of King's Mountain, North Carolina • General Nathanael Greene replaces General Gates

1781

JANUARY Mutiny of the Pennsylvania Line • Battle of Cowpens, South Carolina

FEBRUARY Marquis de Lafayette begins his Virginia Campaign

MARCH Battle of Guilford Court House, North Carolina

MAY Pensacola, Florida, falls to Spanish

SEPTEMBER Battle of the Virginia (Chesapeake) Capes • Battle of Eutaw Springs, South Carolina

OCTOBER Cornwallis surrenders at Yorktown

1782–1783

MARCH 1782 British Prime Minister Lord North resigns and a new government takes power

APRIL 1782 Sir Guy Carleton becomes commander of British forces in America • Washington headquartered at Newburgh, New York

JUNE 1782 British evacuate Savannah

AUGUST 1782 British and American forces fight at Combahee Ferry, South Carolina

NOVEMBER 1782 Preliminary peace treaty is signed between Britain and the United States

DECEMBER 1782 British evacuate Charleston, most troops sail to New York

SEPTEMBER 1783 The Peace of Paris is signed by United States, Great Britian, France, Spain, and the Netherlands

NOVEMBER 1783 Washington enters New York as British evacuate

DECEMBER 1783 George Washington resigns from command of the Continental Army

LIBERATION OF NEW YORK

REVOLUTIONARY AMERICA

Lake Superior

The main British army was at Boston in 1775, where the first clashes of the War for Independence took place.

A Patriot invasion of Canada was defeated by early 1776, but Washington drove the British out of Boston. In the New York campaign that summer, the British shattered Washington's army. The Patriots recovered at Trenton in December, and fought on.

In 1777, the British captured Philadelphia, but a royal army was wiped out at Saratoga. The British abandoned Philadelphia in 1778 and returned to New York, which Washington put under siege.

The war moved to the South in 1779–1780, with British victories at Savannah, Charleston, and Camden. Patriots triumphed at King's Mountain in 1780 and at The Cowpens in 1781. Though the British won the field at Guilford Court House and Eutaw Springs that year, they suffered irreplaceable losses.

In the fall of 1781, the Yorktown campaign saw the French fleet triumph off the Virginia capes. This victory was followed in October by the surrender of Cornwallis to the allied American and French armies.

Lake Michigan

Mississippi River

VINCENNES
(FT. SACKVILLE)

KASKASKIA

AMERICAN CANNONEERS

PENSACOLA

NEW ORLEANS

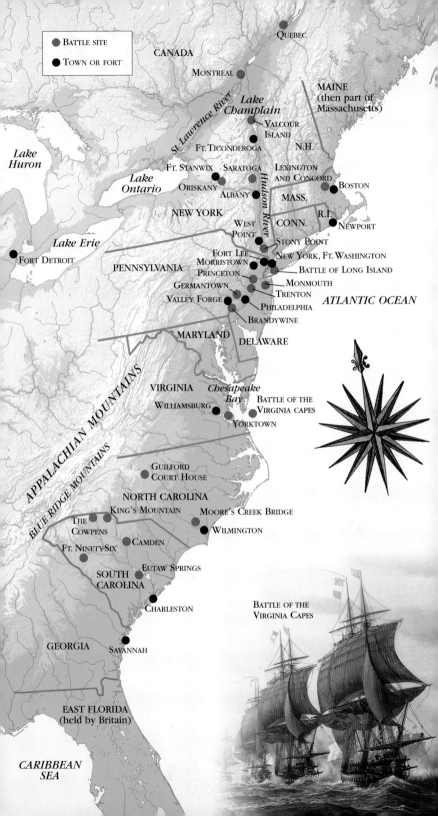

BATTLE SITE
TOWN OR FORT

CANADA

QUEBEC

MONTREAL

MAINE
(then part of
Massachusetts)

St. Lawrence River

Lake Champlain

VALCOUR
ISLAND

FT. TICONDEROGA

N.H.

FT. STANWIX   SARATOGA

Lake Ontario

ORISKANY

ALBANY

Hudson River

LEXINGTON
AND CONCORD

BOSTON

MASS.

NEW YORK

CONN.

R.I.

WEST
POINT

NEWPORT

Lake Huron

STONY POINT

Lake Erie

FORT DETROIT

FORT LEE
MORRISTOWN

NEW YORK, FT. WASHINGTON

BATTLE OF LONG ISLAND

PENNSYLVANIA

PRINCETON

MONMOUTH

GERMANTOWN

TRENTON

VALLEY FORGE

PHILADELPHIA

ATLANTIC OCEAN

BRANDYWINE

MARYLAND

DELAWARE

VIRGINIA

Chesapeake Bay

BATTLE OF THE
VIRGINIA CAPES

WILLIAMSBURG

YORKTOWN

APPALACHIAN MOUNTAINS

GUILFORD
COURT HOUSE

BLUE RIDGE MOUNTAINS

NORTH CAROLINA

KING'S MOUNTAIN

MOORE'S CREEK BRIDGE

THE
COWPENS

WILMINGTON

CAMDEN

FT. NINETY-SIX

EUTAW SPRINGS

SOUTH
CAROLINA

BATTLE OF THE
VIRGINIA CAPES

CHARLESTON

GEORGIA

SAVANNAH

EAST FLORIDA
(held by Britain)

CARIBBEAN SEA

The Fight for
Liberty Begins

In Boston, General Thomas Gage worried that Americans were gathering military stores to use against his soldiers. In April, he sent an expedition to capture guns and ammunition in Concord.

Thousands of Patriots rose up and fought the Regulars at Lexington and Concord, driving them back to Boston. The city was under siege, and the War for Independence had begun.

On May 10, Americans surprised and captured strategic Fort Ticonderoga on Lake Champlain. The fort was taken without a fight by Ethan Allen and his "Green Mountain Boys." They were from the Hampshire Grants, the mountain region east of the fort. Colonel Benedict Arnold of Connecticut also took part in the capture.

In Philadelphia, on June 17, the Continental Congress commissioned

REVERE'S MIDNIGHT RIDE
Before war began, silversmith Paul Revere of Boston rode out several times to warn of British plans to capture militia stores. On April 18, 1775, Revere and other Patriot riders called out the Minutemen to oppose the Regulars marching to Concord.

April	May	June	July
Lexington and Concord	Second Continental	Congress makes George	George Washington takes
Siege of Boston begins	Congress convenes in	Washington commander	charge of American forces
	Philadelphia	of the American Army	at Boston
	Capture of Fort Ticonderoga	Battle of Breed's Hill	

George Washington commander-in-chief of the new American army. That same day, Patriots occupying Breed's Hill at Boston were attacked by Gage's Regulars. The British took the hill after a bloody fight, but the siege continued.

Early in July, Washington took over the siege of Boston. He ordered an invasion of Canada and called for Ticonderoga's cannon to be brought to Boston. Montreal fell in November, but a few weeks later the Americans were defeated at Quebec. Until then, 1775 had been a year of Patriot triumphs.

GRAND UNION FLAG

PARADING THE ARMY

George Washington rode up from Philadelphia and took command at Boston on July 2. His force numbered 17,000 militia, but shrank to a third of that when enlistments were up. Gage had 6,500 "Regulars," as professional troops were termed. On New Year's Day, 1776, Americans raised the Grand Union Flag, one of the first Patriot flags. The 13 stripes are for the colonies; the Union Jack symbolizes America's ties to Britain. The Stars and Stripes became the flag of the United States on June 14, 1777.

INTO A STORM OF BULLETS
Iron discipline keeps the Regulars in tight ranks as they begin another frontal assault on the Patriot fortifications on Breed's Hill. Before the last assault, the soldiers threw off their packs.

COMMANDER-IN-CHIEF
Washington salutes his troops in an idealized picture of his arrival at Boston. Few of his militia volunteers had uniforms. Most wore civilian clothes while serving with the army.

August	September	November	December
King George III issues a proclamation declaring colonies in open rebellion	American invasion of Canada begins	Invading American forces capture St. John's, Canada, then Montreal	American attack on Quebec City fails

MINUTEMEN ROUT REGULARS

On the night of April 18, 1775, 800 elite British troops left Boston and rowed silently across the Charles River. After forming into columns, they headed toward Concord. They were searching for military stores that had been gathered there by local militiamen.

Patriot leader Dr. Joseph Warren heard of the troop movement. He alerted riders Paul Revere and William Dawes to warn the Patriot militia that the British were coming. Also, signal lanterns were hung in Boston's North Church to report how the British were coming: "one [lantern] if by land, two if by sea."

The militia were called "Minutemen" because they were trained to respond instantly to a British move. A company of Minutemen commanded by Captain John Parker blocked the Regulars at the town of Lexington. The first shot of the American Revolution was fired here, although it is unclear who fired it. The Regulars brushed aside Parker's small force and continued to Concord. There, they learned the Patriots' gunpowder and ammunition had already been hidden.

Soon, the Regulars found themselves attacked by thousands of

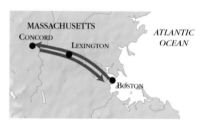

ATTACK AND RETREAT OF BRITISH REGULARS

A FATEFUL JOURNEY
On April 19, 1775, a British expedition marched from Boston to Concord to find military stores. The troops were surrounded by militia and had to fight their way back to Boston.

ATTACKING THE REARGUARD
British Regulars fight their way back to Boston after clashing with Patriots at Lexington and Concord. Americans fired constantly on the withdrawing troops, who sometimes counterattacked with bayonet charges.

Losses	
American:	49 killed, 41 wounded, 5 prisoners/missing
British:	73 killed, 174 wounded

angry militia. The British commander, Lt. Colonel Francis Smith, was wounded. Major John Pitcairn took over and ordered his men back to Boston. The 20-mile (32-kilometer) retreat was a running battle with militia firing from behind stone walls and trees and from inside houses. Reinforcements arrived to cover the retreating Regulars, but the entire British force had to withdraw to Boston.

The militia followed close behind and camped all around Boston. The British-held city was now under siege, and the American Revolution had begun.

WELL-DRESSED VOLUNTEER
This red woolen waistcoat was worn by a militiaman who mustered to confront Regulars near Concord. Militia often wore their best clothes to muster.

THE LEADERSHIP

MASSACHUSETTS MILITIA OFFICERS were civilians, but many were battle-tested in the French and Indian War. The British officers were professional soldiers, yet often were young and inexperienced.

"Don't fire until fired upon. But if they want a war, let it begin here."
—Parker, to his militia company at Lexington Green

JOHN PARKER (1729-1775)
Massachusetts farmer John Parker was a veteran of the French and Indian War. He was elected by his men to be captain of Lexington's militia. Parker blocked the path of the British marching toward Concord. His militiamen later testified that the Regulars fired first, killing eight and wounding ten Americans.

"Stop, you rebels!"
—Pitcairn, to the militia at Lexington Green

JOHN PITCAIRN (1722-1775)
Scottish-born John Pitcairn was a major of the Royal Marines. Pitcairn was well-regarded by most Bostonians. He led the advance column of Regulars to Lexington. Pitcairn was killed a few weeks later in the assault on Breed's Hill. His son was a soldier and fought with him in that battle. Pitcairn's marines said that they had "all lost a father."

THREE BLOODY ASSAULTS

British troops in Boston woke to a rude surprise on the morning of June 17. The heights across the Charles River were swarming with 1,200 Patriot militiamen. British commander Thomas Gage ordered an attack. General Sir William Howe led 2,200 Regulars across the river in barges to capture the defenses. The original American orders had been to fortify Bunker Hill. Rebel general Israel Putnam of Connecticut mistakenly had seized nearby Breed's Hill instead.

Bayonets slanted forward, the scarlet-coated British advanced in perfect formation up Breed's Hill. This was a terrifying sight for the inexperienced American militiamen. But many Patriot officers were seasoned veterans of the French and Indian War. They kept their men steady. When the

Latin motto translates to "Difficulties do not dismay us."

GRENADIER'S FUR CAP
Elite troops in the British Army, the grenadiers were distinguished by their tall fur caps.

READY TO FIGHT
Patriots waiting in the earthworks of Breed's Hill expect the fierce bayonet attack of British Regulars. With determined leaders, the Americans fought off two assaults. They ran out of ammunition in the third British attack and retreated.

Losses	
American:	140 killed, 301 wounded, 30 taken prisoner
British:	226 killed, 924 wounded

British were almost on them, the Rebels fired at point-blank range, mowing down the Regulars. General Howe reformed his shattered ranks, and again the British came on. Again the Americans fired, covering the hillside with scarlet dead. Before the third assault, the Regulars threw down their heavy packs. Then they advanced.

In the face of this desperate charge the Americans ran out of ammunition and retreated. Howe captured Breed's Hill, but it cost him more than 1,000 dead and wounded. The Americans lost about 400. At Breed's Hill, the Patriots learned they could stand against even the best British Regulars.

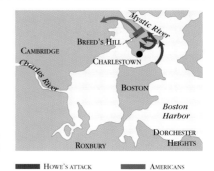

◼◼◼ HOWE'S ATTACK   ◼◼◼ AMERICANS

BREED'S HILL ENGAGEMENT
The Regulars crossed by boat from Boston to the Charleston peninsula, where Patriots had dug in. Gage later was faulted for not cutting off the Americans at the peninsula's neck instead of attacking frontally.

THE LEADERSHIP

GENERAL HOWE EXPECTED the New Englanders on Breed's Hill to run as soon as his soldiers attacked. The senior American commanders, including General Putnam, were resolved to stand and fight.

"When I look to the consequences . . . I do it with horror. Success was too dearly bought."

—Howe, in a report after Breed's Hill

WILLIAM HOWE (1729-1814)
Howe was a nobleman and a general who was adored by the troops. He bravely led the Regulars in the assaults up Breed's Hill. Howe later replaced Gage as overall British commander in America.

"Americans are . . . much afraid for their legs; if you cover these, they will fight forever."

—Putnam, proposing earthworks on Breed's Hill

ISRAEL PUTNAM (1718-1790)
Connecticut's General Putnam was an elderly veteran of the French and Indian War and a recognized hero. Congress named him a general, but he was inexperienced in such a high rank.

WASHINGTON TAKES CHARGE

On July 2, 1775, two weeks after the bloody battle of Breed's Hill, General George Washington rode into the American camp outside Boston. The Continental Congress had named Washington commander-in-chief of the Patriot Army. Through the summer and fall of 1775, Washington struggled to hold the volunteers together. Most wanted to go home to their farms. He had 17,000 men, but the majority of enlistments soon would end. Washington called on his officers to find replacements for those soldiers who went home.

By October, British General Thomas Gage had been removed as commander of the Boston defenders.

The British government was angry about the heavy losses at the Battle of Breed's Hill. Gage was replaced by Sir William Howe.

There was little gunpowder or ammunition available for the Patriot force facing Boston. What Washington most needed, however, were big siege cannon that could fire into the city. Artillery officer Henry Knox proposed getting the guns at Fort Ticonderoga, 300 miles (483 kilometers) away. From December 1775 to January 1776, Knox's men hauled more than 60 cannon and mortars across rivers and

KNOX OVERSEES THE HAUL
It was an almost impossible task, but Henry Knox and his men wrestled heavy cannon from Fort Ticonderoga to Boston in the winter of 1775–1776. From then on, Knox was one of Washington's best commanders.

Losses: Capture of Ft. Ticonderoga	
American:	negligible
British:	50 prisoners

over snowy mountains. They moved the artillery overland on heavy sleds pulled by oxen. The total weight was almost 120,000 pounds (54,432 kilograms), with another 2,300 pounds (1,043 kilograms) of ammunition. Knox described his procession as "a noble train of artillery."

At last, they reached Washington's army at Boston. Washington hoped the British would evacuate and not force him to bombard the city.

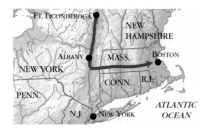

THE ROUTE FROM "TI" TO BOSTON
Washington's army kept Boston under siege as Knox's men slowly pushed and pulled dozens of guns through the winter wilderness.

KNOX'S ROUTE

THE LEADERSHIP

AS HAD MANY BRITISH OFFICERS, Gage served in America much of his career. Washington did not have professional officers like the British, but the Patriots would fight hard defending homes and country.

"I wish this cursed place was burned. The only use is its harbour…but in all other respects it is the worst place to act offensively from, or defensively."

—Gage describes his disgust with occupying Boston

THOMAS GAGE (1721–1787)
General Gage had been a first-rate officer in the French and Indian War. He had an American wife and many friends in the colonies. At first, Gage tried to avoid bloodshed, but anti-British feelings ran too deep in New England.

"It appeared to me almost a miracle that people with heavy loads should be able to get up and down such hills."

—Knox, on the western Massachusetts mountains

HENRY KNOX (1750–1806)
A self-taught artillerist, Knox was a Boston bookseller before the war. He became a key advisor and friend to George Washington, who often depended on Knox at crucial moments during the Revolution.

GUNS ON THE HEIGHTS

On the night of March 4, under a full moon, Washington occupied Dorchester Heights overlooking Boston. More than 1,200 men began fortifying the heights for Knox's cannon.

The workers could not dig into the frozen ground, so they quickly built defenses out of wooden frameworks. These they filled with hay and barrels of dirt hauled to the site by 360 oxcarts. Then the cannon were pulled into position. Now, not only was Boston threatened, but the British ships in the harbor were under Patriot guns. Still, Washington hoped for a bloodless ending to the siege. He waited for Howe to react.

The British commander was dismayed to see the guns on the heights. A bombardment of the city would cause much death and destruction. Yet, Howe did not want to retreat without a fight. He prepared to go on the offensive.

On March 5, Howe ordered an attack against Dorchester Heights. A heavy storm came up, however, making it impossible for the troops to

THE LEADERSHIP

THREE TOP BRITISH GENERALS were besieged in Boston: Howe, Henry Clinton, and John Burgoyne. They led a disciplined, professional force. Washington had to hold together his ill-supplied volunteer army almost singlehandedly.

WILLIAM HOWE (1729-1814)
In October 1775, King George III gave Sir William command of British forces in America. Howe wanted to abandon Boston and capture New York. From there he could better move against the Patriots.

"These fellows have done more work in one night than I could have made my army do in three months."

—Howe sees new Patriot earthworks on Dorchester Heights

"Our situation is truly alarming, and of this General Howe is well apprised . . . ."

—Washington to Congress, worrying about his army's weakness

GEORGE WASHINGTON (1732-1799)
A Virginia plantation owner, Washington won a reputation for courage and leadership in the French and Indian War. Congress elected him overall commander-in-chief to lead the Patriot army at Boston.

cross the bay. Howe called off the assault. He knew now that he must evacuate Boston or be shot to pieces. He warned that he would burn down the city if the Americans tried to stop the evacuation. Washington held his fire.

The British loaded 11,000 military personnel and 1,000 Loyalist civilians into ships. On March 17, the fleet sailed up the coast toward Halifax, Nova Scotia. The eight-month siege was over, and Washington marched into the city.

The fall of Boston was a great victory, although Howe's army had not been captured. The Patriots were left to wonder where the British would strike next. Many

guessed it would be a blow at the center of the colonies, an attack on New York City.

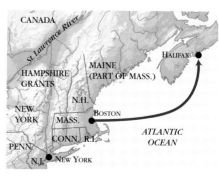

■ BRITISH EVACUATION

HOWE ESCAPES TO CANADA
Howe pulled his troops out of Boston and also evacuated many Loyalist civilians. The British and Loyalists sailed to Halifax, Canada.

Carved wooden plug

POWDER HORN
This Patriot-owned powder horn was sealed and plugged tightly to keep gunpowder dry so it would ignite when fired in a musket. It was carried by a soldier during the Siege of Boston.

"In Defense of Liberty" is carved into horn

GUNS THREATEN BOSTON
Washington studies the British defenses of Boston with a spyglass while his men dig artillery positions on Dorchester Heights. The risk of bombardment soon forced Howe and his army to evacuate the city.

Losses: Siege of Boston	
American:	20 killed
British:	43 killed/wounded/prisoners

PATRIOTS MARCH ON CANADA

Many Americans believed if the British troops in Canada were defeated, the Canadians would join the Revolution. General Schuyler gathered soldiers and supplies for an invasion of Canada. In late August, his force started north on Lake Champlain.

A strong British fort at St. Johns, guarding the route to Montreal, held out for months. During the siege, Schuyler fell ill, and General Richard Montgomery of New York took command. St. Johns surrendered in November, and the way to Montreal was open. Moving quickly north, Montgomery easily captured the city.

To defend Canada, British Governor Guy Carleton had only 800 Regulars. Most of this force was lost in the surrender of St. Johns. Yet the resistance there gave Carleton time to scrape together enough men to defend Quebec City, which was then the capital of Canada.

By now, Washington had ordered Colonel Benedict Arnold to make a

THE LEADERSHIP

MILITARY COMMANDERS in the northern provinces of New York, New England, and Canada had to be excellent diplomats. These leaders tried to win the support of French Canadians, native peoples, and settlers of British, Dutch, Irish, and German heritage.

GUY CARLETON (1724–1808)
Governor of Canada and a war veteran, Sir Guy was one of the most respected leaders in America. He refused to give up Quebec City to the Patriots, even though his force was outnumbered.

"The messenger was sent to prison for a few days and drummed out [of town]."
—Carleton's response to a demand for Quebec's surrender

PHILIP SCHUYLER (1733–1804)
A wealthy landowner of upper New York, General Schuyler rallied settlers to the Patriot cause. He was often ill, but worked hard to keep his army together. Schuyler was respected by the Indians and was a strong supporter of Washington.

"Not one earthly thing for offense or defense has been done [at Ticonderoga, which is in] a perfectly defenseless state."
—Schuyler describes the ruined fort he must repair

second invasion of Canada. Arnold left Boston in September with 1,100 men, heading for Quebec. The Americans made a 350-mile (563-kilometer) march northward through the Maine wilderness. They endured a fierce hurricane and bitterly cold weather. Running out of food, they lost many deserters, who turned back. Only 675 men reached Quebec that November, to camp under the high fortress walls. Montgomery's force soon joined them, and he took command.

The Patriots called for Carleton to surrender, but he refused. Montgomery had no artillery to pound the city. He would have to launch an assault.

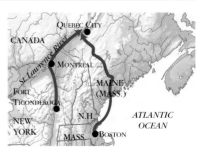

AMERICAN ROUTE OF INVASION

INVASION OF CANADA
Patriots led by Richard Montgomery captured Montreal and moved on toward Quebec City. Others, under Benedict Arnold, invaded through Maine.

PATRIOT LEADER'S SWORD
This sword belonged to an officer in the Canada invasion. It is decorated with a lion's head and the words: "God Bless the Province of New York."

GRIM CAMPAIGNERS
Arnold's weary fighters slog through the northern forest toward Quebec. The weather was cold and wet, the wilderness dense and rugged. After six weeks, the Americans finally reached the walls of the city.

Losses: Canadian Campaign	
American:	550 killed/wounded/missing
British:	1,689 killed/wounded/missing

REPULSE AND RETREAT

In December 1775, Montgomery and Arnold were camped outside Quebec with about 1,000 men. Inside the city, Governor Carleton and Lieutenant Colonel Allan Maclean had a force of 1,800 Regulars, Loyalists, and militia.

At midnight on December 31, the Americans moved out during a howling snowstorm. Montgomery and Arnold assaulted Quebec from two sides. Arnold's attack broke through. His men scrambled on scaling ladders up and over the icy fortress walls. While leading his troops, Arnold was wounded and had to be carried back to the American camp. Captain Daniel Morgan, a Virginian, took over Arnold's command. Morgan continued the attack, reaching a barricade in the inner city.

At the other end of town, Montgomery was killed by a surprise blast of cannon fire. His men lost heart and retreated. Morgan's force was left

THE LEADERSHIP

GENERAL JOHN THOMAS OF MASSACHUSETTS, a veteran of the French and Indian War, took command of Patriot forces at Quebec in the spring. Thomas died of smallpox, and Sullivan took charge.

"Maclean . . . was indefatigable [as a commander]."

—A British officer's report from Quebec

ALLAN MACLEAN (1725-1797)
Lieutenant Colonel Maclean, a Scot, was a veteran of the French and Indian War. He recruited Scottish settlers for the Loyalist regiment known as the Royal Highland Emigrants. Maclean was second in command at Quebec and later became a brigadier general.

"I don't want anything to lower my spirits. I have abundant use for them all, and at the best of times I have not too much."

—Montgomery tells his wife not to write him "whining" letters

**RICHARD MONTGOMERY
(1738-1775)**
A retired Regular officer, the Irish-born General Montgomery left his Hudson Valley estate to join the Patriots. He was a dashing figure, always at the forefront of his troops. Advancing through a snowstorm at Quebec, he was killed by the blast of an enemy cannon.

SCOTTISH THISTLE
This heart-shaped belt piece with a thistle motif belonged to a sergeant of the Royal Highland Regiment. The thistle is a traditional symbol of Scotland.

alone inside the city walls. The defenders quickly surrounded them, forcing Morgan to surrender.

The siege continued, but spring brought a huge fleet with British reinforcements sailing up the St. Lawrence. Carleton soon drove the Rebel forces from Quebec, then recaptured Montreal and St. Johns. The Americans withdrew southward, suffering from a smallpox epidemic that swept through their camps.

Holding out on Lake Champlain, Arnold's force still hoped to stop Carleton from capturing strategic Fort Ticonderoga.

In June, General John Sullivan brought American reinforcements and took command of the American forces. More than 3,000 of his troops were gravely ill with smallpox. He organized a withdrawal southward to Crown Point on Lake Champlain. There, General Horatio Gates arrived to take over the army and prepare to withstand Carleton's invasion.

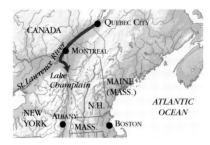

CARLETON'S ROUTE

CARLETON'S PURSUIT
With the coming of spring, Carleton drove the Americans up the St. Lawrence River and south on Lake Champlain. Arnold regrouped his forces and began building a small fleet, hoping to stop Carleton on Lake Champlain.

DEATH IN THE SNOW
General Montgomery and his closest officers led the advance along a narrow Quebec City lane on the last day of 1775. They were concealed by swirling snow until spotted by surprised defenders of an enemy blockhouse. The British fired a cannon before fleeing. That chance shot killed Montgomery, who is shown falling, mortally wounded.

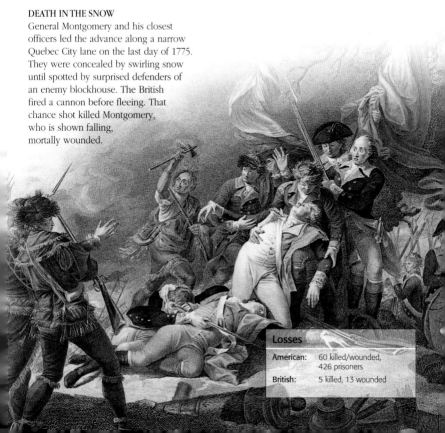

Losses	
American:	60 killed/wounded, 426 prisoners
British:	5 killed, 13 wounded

Independence, Retreat, and Rally

The first half of 1776 went well for the Patriots as General Howe was driven from Boston in March. Another victory came in June, when the Royal Navy's attack on Charleston, South Carolina, was repulsed.

The main concern for the Patriots was in Canada, where Governor Carleton recaptured Montreal.

In the hopeful days of July 1776, the Continental Congress passed the Declaration of Independence from Britain. The Revolution was in danger, however. Howe had sailed into New York harbor with hundreds of ships and 32,000 Regulars. At the Battle of Long Island in August, he defeated Washington, whose army was trapped against the East River. To Howe's dismay, Washington's army escaped, rowing across the river through a thick fog. New York City soon fell to the British Army and Howe.

Defeat was in the air by that fall. In October, the British destroyed a Rebel fleet at Valcour Island on Lake

A CITY IN FLAMES
Patriots tried to burn down New York to keep the enemy from occupying it. The fires were put out, however, and the British settled in for the rest of the war.

February	June	July	August
Battle of Moore's Creek Bridge, North Carolina	Siege of Charleston (1st)	Declaration of Independence is signed	Battle of Long Island
		Howe's fleet arrives in New York Harbor	Washington evacuates Brooklyn

Champlain. Washington's battered army was driven from New York and retreated through New Jersey. Enlistments were expiring. Most of his soldiers would be going home at the start of 1777.

In this dark hour, Washington needed a victory or he would have no army left. On Christmas Day, he led his troops across the ice-choked Delaware River and defeated the Hessian garrison at Trenton, New Jersey.

This triumph gave the Americans new hope. Many men reenlisted to continue serving with Washington, who had won their respect. The army and the Revolution had survived another year.

RETREAT TO FIGHT AGAIN
After several disastrous defeats around New York, Washington hurried the remainder of his army across New Jersey. Late in the year, he crossed the Delaware River, preparing to oppose any British attack on Philadelphia.

A NEW NATION RISES

In mid-1776, delegates to the Continental Congress in Philadelphia were encouraged by the victories at Boston and Charleston. Virginia's Thomas Jefferson led a congressional committee that drafted the Declaration of Independence. There was no way back to colonial days. Congress adopted the Declaration on July 4.

The 13 former colonies now were 13 independent states, formally allied against the mighty British Empire. Congressional delegates used this ink stand to sign the Declaration of Independence.

SILVER INK STAND

LIBERTY'S CALL
Jefferson rewrote the Declaration several times before it was finally ready for adoption by Congress.

September	October	November	December
Battle of Harlem Heights	Battle of Valcour Island	Fall of Fort Washington and Fort Lee	Battle of Trenton, New Jersey
Great Fire of New York	Battle of White Plains, New York	Washington retreats through New Jersey	

Battle of Moore's Creek Bridge, February 1776

NEIGHBOR AGAINST NEIGHBOR

After Lexington and Concord, North Carolina Patriots prepared for a fight of their own. The colony's Loyalists also organized for a struggle. North Carolina was evenly divided between Patriots, who supported Congress, and supporters of the king.

General Gage sent Scottish-born General Donald McDonald and Colonel Donald McLeod to North Carolina. They rallied many Scots to support the royal governor, Josiah Martin. In mid-February, news came of a British expedition sailing to capture Charleston. General McDonald led a force of almost 1,800 men toward the coast to join this expedition. McDonald fell ill, but his troops marched on. Many wore traditional highland kilts and carried the Scottish broadsword.

James Moore, leader of Patriot troops in North Carolina, decided to stop the Loyalists. The 650 men of his 1st North Carolina Continental regiment were reinforced by hundreds of Patriot volunteers. Moore sent 1,000 men under ranger Richard Caswell to hold the bridge over Moore's Creek.

At dawn on February 27, Colonel McLeod and Loyalist captain John Campbell led a rush to take the bridge. The pipes skirled fiercely and the Scots shouted the battle cry, "King George and broadswords!" The Patriots were waiting for them. Cannon fire mowed the attackers down, killing McLeod and Campbell. A Patriot counterattack threw the Loyalists back in confusion, and they fled. Patriot forces blocking their escape captured many of them.

HIGHLAND SWORD
Scottish fighting men traditionally carried broadswords into battle, but they were no match for artillery fire.

PATRIOTS AMBUSH LOYAL SCOTS
The march of North Carolina Loyalists of Scottish descent was stopped by a burst of Patriot cannon fire at Moore's Creek Bridge. The leaders were shot down, and most of the men were captured.

Losses	
Patriot:	1 killed, 1 wounded
Loyalist:	50 killed/wounded, 850 prisoners/missing

General McDonald and more than 850 Loyalists were taken prisoner. The Patriots went through the countryside, arresting known Tory sympathizers and taking the weapons owned by their families. Governor Martin fled the colony, as did many Loyalists. Despite the hard feelings on both sides, the prisoners were treated with respect. This helped convince many not to take up arms against the Patriots again.

The lack of a cooperating Loyalist force in coastal North Carolina became a setback for the British in the approaching Charleston Expedition.

■■■ BRITISH AND LOYALIST FORCES

■■■ PATRIOT FORCES

A FAILED CAMPAIGN
Clinton's expedition against Charleston was to support Loyalists, who were marching to the coast. The Loyalists were cut off and captured before they could meet Clinton's army.

THE LEADERSHIP

THE LOYALISTS WERE LED by Colonel Donald McLeod, sent by Gage to Governor Moore. Loyalist John Campbell led the advance guard. Patriot colonel Richard Caswell commanded 800 rangers.

JAMES MOORE (1737-1777)
Colonel Moore had served in the French and Indian War. He opposed the Stamp Act and in 1776 joined the Sons of Liberty. As commander of the 1st North Carolina Continentals, he organized the campaign that won the battle at Moore's Creek Bridge.

"This, we think, will effectually put a stop to [Loyalists] in North Carolina."

—A pro-Patriot newspaper report of the battle

JOSIAH MARTIN (1737-1786)
North Carolina's royal governor, Martin was a former British officer. After the Loyalists were defeated at Moore's Creek, he escaped on a British warship. He joined Clinton at Charleston in 1779 and served with Cornwallis in the Carolinas.

"[This is the moment] when this country might be delivered from anarchy...."

—Governor Martin, expecting a North Carolina Loyalist victory

CAROLINA GUNS ROAR

In January, the British government ordered General Sir Henry Clinton to take control of Virginia, North and South Carolina, and Georgia. Commodore Peter Parker commanded the fleet transporting Clinton's army. The leaders planned first to capture Charleston, South Carolina, the region's leading port city.

On June 4, British ships sailed into sight of Charleston. Defending the harbor were new American forts on Sullivan's Island and James Island. On Sullivan, Patriot officer William Moultrie was in charge of a half-finished fort of palmetto logs and sand. No one knew if the fort could hold up against a bombardment by British naval guns. Yet Moultrie, who was short of ammunition, was determined not to retreat.

On June 28, the royal ships moved into range to pound the Rebel positions with cannon fire. A hundred British naval guns filled the air with flying metal, but the spongy palmetto wood absorbed the force of the cannonballs. The Americans returned fire skillfully. They conserved gunpowder and made each shot count. The enemy ships were hit many times and badly damaged. Then three warships ran aground, and Commodore Parker himself was

COOLNESS UNDER FIRE
British warships pound Patriot defenses on Sullivan's Island near Charleston. Aboard the ships it was far worse. American cannons killed many sailors and blasted holes in the British vessels.

Losses	
American:	17 killed, 20 wounded
British:	74 killed, 131 wounded

wounded. That night, Clinton gave up the attack on the forts.

This action at Charleston lifted American spirits. The South had been successfully defended and would not be attacked again for three more years. Loyalists were kept down in the South, where Patriots dominated. When the British invaded, however, Loyalists would rise and fight again.

CLINTON AND PARKER

CRUEL MISSILE
Fired from cannons, chain shot spun and whirled through the air. It tore bodies apart and could destroy the sails of an enemy ship.

A DEFIANT FORT
Colonel Moultrie's earthworks on Sullivan's Island withstood Parker's bombardments. Patriot guns prevented the British from getting a foothold on land near Charleston.

Half cannonballs connected by chain

THE LEADERSHIP

CAPTAIN PARKER'S SHIPS TRANSPORTED Sir Henry Clinton and Lord Charles Cornwallis and their troops. Patriot leaders were General Charles Lee and South Carolina Congressional delegate John Rutledge.

WILLIAM MOULTRIE (1730-1805)
Colonel Moultrie's own family was divided by the war. His brother was the Loyalist governor of East Florida. As the British prepared to attack Charleston, Moultrie disagreed with commanding officer, General Lee, who said Sullivan's Island could not be defended.

"Never did men fight more bravely, and never were men more cool."
—Moultrie, after repulsing the British fleet

PETER PARKER (1721-1811)
Captain Parker fired 7,000 cannonballs at Moultrie's fort, with little effect. The British suffered losses, however, and Parker was wounded. He later was knighted for bravery in the battle and promoted to admiral.

"Not worth mentioning..."
—Parker's alleged reply when told he had leg wounds

BRITISH TAKE NEW YORK

Lower New York Bay was thick with wooden masts from hundreds of British warships in July 1776. This powerful fleet carried an army of 32,000 men. Commanding general Sir William Howe planned to take New York City and gain control of the strategic Hudson River.

Howe landed his troops on Long Island, where Washington's army was positioned at Brooklyn. On the night of August 26, British general Sir Henry Clinton sent a strong force around the Patriot defenses. At dawn, these troops attacked and crushed the left wing of the American army. The Rebels were driven back.

Only a rear-guard of Delaware and Maryland Continentals held out. Their commander, General William Alexander, led a daring counterattack. His men smashed into the British, stopping the advance. Although Alexander's troops soon were overwhelmed, their courage gave the Rebel army time to retreat to new defenses. Now, however, the Americans were trapped against the East River. It seemed Howe would destroy Washington's

OFFICER'S BUTTON
A brass button from the coat of an officer in the Delaware Regiment at Long Island.

"DR" for "Delaware Regiment"

DESPERATE RETREAT
Washington's army escapes across Gowanus Creek as Marylanders hold off Howe's army. The Patriots regrouped at Brooklyn Heights. Then, under cover of darkness, they slipped away before Howe could attack again.

Losses	
American:	1,687 killed/wounded/missing
British/German:	858 killed/wounded/missing

army and end the war.

Then, on the night of August 29, Washington conducted a withdrawal. Under cover of dense fog, 9,500 Americans were ferried silently across to Manhattan without alerting the British. Howe lost his opportunity for a decisive victory, but he soon captured New York. Washington's brilliant escape from the Long Island defeat allowed the Revolutionaries to fight on.

Howe attacked Manhattan. Patriots repelled his troops at Harlem Heights, but Washington had to keep retreating.

ROUTING THE PATRIOTS

The British landed at Staten Island before invading Long Island. After his victory there, Howe pushed on to Manhattan, which he captured in mid-September after some sharp fighting. He next defeated the Patriots at White Plains, New York.

▬▬ HOWE'S ATTACK

▬▬ WASHINGTON

THE LEADERSHIP

GENERAL HOWE HAD excellent commanders: Cornwallis, Clinton, and German generals Philip von Heister and Baron Wilhelm von Knyphausen. Washington's best general, Nathanael Greene, fell ill before the battle. This was a serious loss to the Patriots.

"Is there no way of treading back this step of Independency?"

—Howe to Benjamin Franklin during a meeting to discuss peace

RICHARD HOWE (1726-1799)
Admiral Lord Howe was the brother of General Sir William Howe. The Howes hoped to end the war by negotiation. King George authorized them to be peace commissioners, but the Patriots refused their terms. Lord Howe later became a hero in the Napoleonic Wars.

"[The Regulars are] through the woods and already on this side of the main hills..."

—Stirling in dismay about the enemy's quick advance

WILLIAM ALEXANDER (1726-1783)
Alexander claimed to be Lord Stirling, Scottish nobility. His rebellious father had fled Scotland years before. On Long Island, Stirling led Delaware and Maryland troops who slowed the enemy advance. He was captured, later exchanged, and rejoined Washington.

ARNOLD'S GALLANT FLEET

Governor Carleton pursued the Patriots southward over Lake Champlain. He hoped to retake Fort Ticonderoga then invade down the

> *"I was obliged myself to point most of the guns on board the* Congress, *which I believe did good execution."*

—Arnold to Schuyler after The Battle of Valcour Island

INVASION STOPPED
Carleton moved swiftly southward until checked by Arnold's fleet at Valcour Bay; the British advance was ended by the onset of cold weather.

▬▬▬▬ CARLETON

Hudson River. Guarding Lake Champlain were 15 small vessels commanded by Benedict Arnold. He had hurriedly built his squadron as the British approached. Carleton paused to build a fleet of his own. In a two-day battle starting on October 12, he attacked the outgunned Americans near Valcour Island. Arnold himself manned a cannon after the gunners were killed. His men fought desperately, but almost all their boats were sunk or taken. Carleton won decisively, yet lost too much time. With the harsh northern winter approaching fast, the British army returned to Canada.

THE LEADERSHIP

WITH CARLETON WAS GENERAL JOHN BURGOYNE, who thought the British should have taken Ticonderoga. Philip Schuyler was overall Patriot leader. Arnold was his best officer.

BENEDICT ARNOLD (1741–1801)
Arnold, from Connecticut, was a merchant ship captain. He organized the swift construction of small vessels to fight for control of Champlain. Arnold's flagship was the *Congress*.

Bar shot spun wildly, ripping apart whatever it struck.

Losses

American:	80 killed/wounded, 110 prisoners/missing
British:	40 killed/wounded

BRITISH BAR SHOT

RUN AGROUND
Arnold's 15 vessels were badly shot up by the superior British fleet at Valcour Island. Some boats that survived the battle were leaking. They had to be run up onto the shore before they sank.

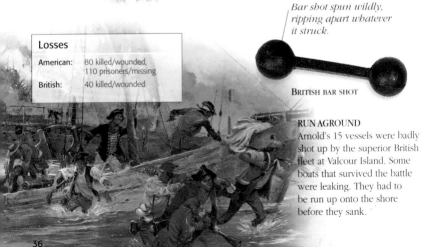

A STRONGHOLD FALLS

When Washington evacuated New York City, he left two forts to hold the Hudson. Fort Washington was on the cliffs of northern Manhattan, and Fort Lee was across the river in New Jersey. They could fire down at British ships.

On November 15, Howe sent 8,000 troops to attack Fort Washington. Hessian general Baron Wilhelm von Knyphausen led the assault. Knyphausen's men charged up the cliffs and forced the Patriots to surrender. The Americans lost 3,000 men and a massive supply of military equipment. A few days later, Fort Lee was abandoned. The loss of men, cannon, and military stores was a devastating blow to the Patriots. Howe now controlled the lower Hudson River.

HOWE
AMERICANS

FT. WASHINGTON CAPTURED
Forts Washington and Lee commanded the Hudson River. Howe proved they were vulnerable to attack by well-trained soldiers.

"Thus the Hessians took possession of the fort [which would] be called Fort Knyphausen."

—from a German soldier's journal

THE LEADERSHIP

GENERAL NATHANAEL GREENE WAS AT FORT LEE, and Colonel Robert Magaw commanded Fort Washington. The Hessians were led by Von Knyphausen and Colonel Johann Rall.

WILHELM VON KNYPHAUSEN (1716–1800)

General von Knyphausen accepted the surrender of Fort Washington. The fort was renamed Fort Knyphausen. He later became commander of German troops in America and fought with distinction in the battles of Brandywine, Germantown, and Monmouth.

ROYAL NAVY ON THE HUDSON
British warships sail north under fire from Fort Lee on the west bank of the Hudson River. Patriot gunners in Fort Lee and Fort Washington, on the opposite bank, could not stop the Royal Navy from sailing up the river.

Losses	
American:	53 killed, 2,818 wounded/prisoners
British/German:	78 killed, 374 wounded

VICTORY IN A DARK HOUR

New York had fallen, and Washington's army was in full retreat through New Jersey. Close behind came the British army. Washington reached the Delaware River first and crossed over to Pennsylvania. He gathered up all the boats on the river to keep the enemy from following.

General Howe was sure Washington would be easily destroyed when spring came. Howe set up a chain of forts from New York through New Jersey and settled down for winter. In the post closest to the enemy was a Hessian brigade under Colonel Johann von Rall. Rall had little respect for American troops. He was warned that Washington might be planning a surprise attack on the night of December 25, but he continued with Christmas celebrations.

In the early morning of December 26, the American assault exploded on Trenton. Washington had crossed the Delaware that night through driving

THE LEADERSHIP

THE HESSIAN OFFICERS BECAME OVERCONFIDENT after the easy victories at New York. Washington, on the other hand, was desperate to win a battle. Before the fight, he scribbled on a paper: "Victory or Death."

"Let them come. We need no trenches. We will go at them with the bayonet."

—Rall's reply when warned Americans might attack

JOHANN VON RALL (C. 1720–1776)
Colonel Rall held his ground at Trenton until fatally wounded. Though dying, he had the dignity to stand before Washington and surrender his sword. After the defeat, Rall was accused of neglect of duty.

"These are the times that try men's souls."

—Soldier Tom Paine, with Washington's army

JOHN GLOVER (1732–1797)
Colonel Glover commanded fishermen from Marblehead, Massachusetts. They ferried the defeated Patriot army off Long Island. Next they took charge of Washington's Delaware crossing at Trenton—and the return trip. Glover later rose to general.

sleet and snow. Patriot gunpowder was soaked, so the soldiers had to attack with only their bayonets. General Knox's artillery was effective, however. It raked the surprised Hessians as they rushed into the streets. Rall was mortally wounded in the quick, furious fight. The Hessian commander, who was dying, surrendered his sword to Washington.

The Patriots immediately recrossed the Delaware with 900 Hessian prisoners. Crossing and recrossing the river were extremely difficult achievements, managed by boatmen from Marblehead, Massachusetts. The victory brought hope to the American army. Many men due to go home agreed to reenlist as a result.

Delaware River

WASHINGTON'S CROSSING

PRINCETON

NEWTOWN

NEW JERSEY

TRENTON

PENNSYLVANIA

▬▬ AMERICAN ATTACK

A DARING PLAN
Washington attacked Trenton from two directions. Another Patriot force downstream could not get across the ice-choked river and stayed on the Pennsylvania side.

HESSIAN FUSILIER CAP
This hat was called a "mitre" cap because it resembled a headpiece worn by bishops. It belonged to a member of the Regiment von Knyphausen. A lion decorates its front plate.

HAZARDOUS ICE FLOES
Washington surely did not stand up in the boat when he crossed the Delaware. His men had to paddle through chunks of ice, as shown. Snow, sleet, and hail helped conceal their approach, but the Patriots suffered in the subzero weather—two even froze to death.

Losses	
American:	negligible
German:	22 killed, 918 wounded/prisoners/missing

A Year of
Great Battles

By early January 1777, Washington's army had crossed back to the east side of the Delaware River. British general Charles Cornwallis moved in and almost trapped Washington.

As at Long Island, the Americans escaped in the night, leaving Cornwallis empty-handed. Next, they surprised and defeated part of Cornwallis's force at Princeton, New Jersey. Afterward, Washington moved his army into winter quarters at Morristown, New Jersey.

That June, a royal army under General John Burgoyne sailed southward over Lake Champlain. Burgoyne captured Fort Ticonderoga, which the Patriots had abandoned. He planned to march to Albany, expecting to meet Howe's main army sailing up the Hudson River.

Unknown to Burgoyne, Howe had other ideas. He intended to capture Philadelphia, the American capital. In September, Howe defeated

FAILURE AND PRIDE
Americans unsuccessfully attack the Chew House, a British strongpoint during the Battle of Germantown. Although the Patriots finally retreated, they fought well and almost won.

January	June	July	August
Battle of Princeton	Burgoyne begins an invasion south from Canada	Burgoyne recaptures Fort Ticonderoga	Battle of Oriskany
Washington's army goes into winter quarters at Morristown		Battle of Hubbardton, Vermont	Battle of Bennington

Washington's army at Brandywine, Pennsylvania, and took Philadelphia. In October, Washington attacked the British camps at Germantown, Pennsylvania. After early success, the Americans were repulsed. Yet the Battle of Germantown showed the Patriot army was still strong.

As the Philadelphia campaign raged, Burgoyne's army struggled. Americans destroyed part of his force near Bennington, Vermont. Soon, Burgoyne was surrounded by an army commanded by Horatio Gates. After bitter fighting at Saratoga, Burgoyne surrendered to Gates on October 17.

Now the French government decided to support the Patriots. The American Revolution became a world war.

GENTLEMAN JOHNNY SURRENDERS
General Horatio Gates, center, accepts the sword of General John Burgoyne after the Patriot victory at Saratoga. Prominently shown is frontiersman Daniel Morgan, in white.

WILDERNESS WAR

Fighting between whites and Indians raged along the frontier. Some of the worst was in the Kentucky region. Patriot frontiersman Daniel Boone built Boonesboro, a fort surrounded by wooden walls. The settlement was on the "Wilderness Road" that Boone had helped cut through the forest. Virginia claimed Kentucky, but native peoples considered it their hunting grounds. Whites and Indians began to fight for it. British officers often accompanied the Indian war parties.

Daniel Boone's rifle

KENTUCKY RIFLEMEN
Kentucky hunters were excellent shots with their Pennsylvania-made rifles. They fought "Indian-style," shooting from behind cover, and moving silently through the deep forest.

September	October	November	December
Battle of Brandywine	Battle of Germantown	Congress adopts Articles of Confederation as basis for the government of the United States of America	Washington's army goes into winter quarters at Valley Forge, Pennsylvania
Philadelphia falls to Howe	Burgoyne surrenders after Second Battle of Saratoga		
First Battle of Saratoga			

A SUDDEN, DARING TRIUMPH

On New Year's Day 1777, Washington again crossed the Delaware River to strike at the British. Then, on the evening of January 2, Washington's 5,000 men found themselves facing 8,000 British Regulars under General Charles Cornwallis. The Patriots were pinned against the Delaware River. Cornwallis was sure he had finally trapped Washington.

As at Long Island, Washington made plans to escape in the night. To fool the British, a few men were left behind to stoke campfires. They also pretended to work on defenses with picks and shovels. The main army slipped past Cornwallis and headed for Princeton, a few miles away. There, the advance guard clashed with part of Cornwallis's army. At first the Regulars drove the Americans back in confusion. Then Washington rode into the thick of the battle and rallied his troops. When the main Continental army came up, the British were beaten.

Cornwallis approached for another

Firing mechanism

9-inch (23-centimeter) barrel

PATRIOTS STING CORNWALLIS
The Battle of Princeton raged around the college town. Skillful use of cannon helped the Rebels win the day before withdrawing to winter quarters. In one British counterattack, Patriot general Hugh Mercer was mortally wounded.

DRAGOON PISTOL
A standard pistol carried by British cavalry. This one belonged to the 16th Light Dragoons, who were near Princeton during the battle.

Losses	
American:	40 killed/wounded
British:	60 killed/wounded, 244 prisoners/missing

battle, but the Americans were exhausted from hard marching and fighting. Washington pushed into northern New Jersey to set up a winter camp for the army in the Morristown hills. From that natural stronghold, the Patriots could continue with their daring attacks, as they did at Trenton and Princeton. Those victories and Washington's strong position at Morristown forced Howe to abandon most of New Jersey to the Patriots.

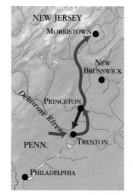

PRINCETON
The American army moved out at night, silently filing around the unsuspecting Cornwallis. The Patriots surprised and attacked a detachment of his force at Princeton.

 CORNWALLIS
WASHINGTON

THE LEADERSHIP

WASHINGTON'S BEST OFFICERS BEGAN to show their ability. Captain Alexander Hamilton was a fine artillerist, and General Hugh Mercer was a promising field leader. Colonel Charles Mahwood commanded the British rear guard attacked by Washington at Princeton.

"Retreat!"

—Mercer's dying "command in a tone of distress," a soldier recalled

HUGH MERCER (1725–1777)
A native Scot, Mercer was a trained medical doctor who lived in Virginia. After emigrating to America, he fought in the French and Indian War and was a friend of Washington's. Mercer helped plan the strategy for the Princeton victory, in which he was killed.

"[We shall] bag the fox."

—Cornwallis, expecting to trap Washington near Trenton

CHARLES CORNWALLIS (1738–1805)
One of the best British commanders, General Cornwallis canceled home leave to pursue Washington. "Wallis," as he was nicknamed, was outmaneuvered and his rear guard defeated as the Patriot army escaped. The British high command said he had blundered.

43

BURGOYNE'S SPLENDID ARMY

General John Burgoyne won the personal approval of King George III for a plan to invade New York from three directions. Burgoyne would move south from Canada to the Hudson River and capture Albany. Lieutenant Colonel Barry St. Leger would come east through the Mohawk Valley. General Howe would sail north up the Hudson River from New York City. These forces would meet at Albany, smashing whoever tried to stop them.

In June, Burgoyne left Canada with 8,000 British, Germans, and Loyalists and a few hundred Indian warriors. His army had

excellent troops and top officers. He was aided by General Simon Fraser, one of the most experienced commanders in America. The Germans under General Baron von Riedesel also were well led. Early in July, Burgoyne found once-powerful Fort Ticonderoga abandoned. He was overjoyed because he had worried about being delayed in a siege of Ticonderoga.

Then Burgoyne's campaign became difficult. Patriot general Philip Schuyler raised the militia to fight the royal forces wherever they were found. St. Leger's advance on the Mohawk was stopped in early August. Later

Gilt device of Brunswick-Wolfenbuttel

SILVER GORGET
A sign of rank, a gorget was suspended from an officer's neck. This gorget is from Brunswick-Wolfenbuttel, a German principality that sent troops to the British.

BATTLE OF BENNINGTON
John Stark's militiamen storm Hessian gunners and dragoons. The German column was ambushed on the march to Bennington. The actual battle took place in Hoosic Falls, New York, west of Bennington.

Losses: First Saratoga phase	
American:	65 killed, 218 wounded, 36 prisoners/missing
British/German:	600 killed/wounded/prisoners/missing

that month, more than 700 German troops advancing on Bennington were wiped out. This force was defeated by militia under General John Stark. More bad news came when Burgoyne learned that Howe was planning to attack Philadelphia and would not come north.

Still, Burgoyne refused to admit failure. He pushed on toward Albany. Unfortunately for him, he had moved too slowly. A Patriot army stood in his path.

CAMPAIGN PLAN
Burgoyne's plan was to move down Lake Champlain, then overland to the Hudson River. St. Leger was to come east from Ft. Oswego to join him at Albany. Howe would strike north from New York City.

▬▬▬ BRITISH FORCES

THE LEADERSHIP

BURGOYNE HAD EXCELLENT GENERALS in Simon Fraser and the German Friedrich von Riedesel. Unfortunately, he did not listen to their advice. Horatio Gates had proven officers in Arnold, ranger leader Daniel Morgan, and New York general Philip van Cortlandt.

"The great bulk of the country is undoubtedly with the Congress."

—Burgoyne, surprised that Loyalists were not joining his army

JOHN BURGOYNE (1722–1792)
General Burgoyne won a reputation leading English dragoons in Spain. He was a ladies' man and a talented playwright. Although Burgoyne convinced King George to launch a northern invasion, his generalship was not up to the ambitious plan he made.

"[T]hat the famous... Burgoyne...should hire the savages of America to scalp Europeans ... is more than will be believed in Europe...."

—Gates to Burgoyne, regarding Indian raids

HORATIO GATES (1728–1806)
Famed as the victor of Saratoga, Gates hoped to replace Washington as commander-in-chief. He was a poor field general, however, as shown at Camden. The English-born Gates had served in the British Army.

Battle of Oriskany, August 1777

BLOODY FRONTIER CLASH

The Mohawk River Valley in central New York was the scene of vicious border warfare during the Revolution. Loyalist and Patriot neighbors battled each other. Led by Mohawk war chief Joseph Brant, powerful Iroquois tribes allied with the Loyalists.

In July, a force of 2,000 Regulars, Loyalists, and Iroquois paddled east on the Mohawk River. Commanded by Lieutenant Colonel Barry St. Leger, it was to join Burgoyne at Albany.

Defending the Patriot settlements of the Mohawk Valley was Fort Stanwix, with 750 troops under Colonel Peter Gansevoort. St. Leger reached the fort on August 2 and

surrounded it, beginning a siege.

To relieve the fort came 800 Mohawk Valley farmers commanded by militia general Nicholas Herkimer. On the morning of August 6, Herkimer marched into a trap just a few miles from the fort. Iroquois and Loyalists ambushed the militia in a narrow ravine. Herkimer and many Patriot

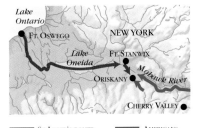

MARCHING TO BURGOYNE
St. Leger's route of advance was along waterways. Fort Stanwix blocked his path down the Mohawk River. At Oriskany, Herkimer's militia checked St. Leger's invasion. Arnold came from Albany to break the siege.

HERKIMER FIGHTS TO THE END
Wounded militia general Nicholas Herkimer directs his men at Oriskany. Loyalist Iroquois and whites laid the ambush. Many were from this same region and were peacetime acquaintances of the Patriots. Herkimer died a few days later.

Losses	
Patriot:	160 killed, 50 wounded/missing
Loyalist/Indian:	150 killed/wounded

officers were immediately cut down. The tough farmers rallied and charged the enemy, fighting hand to hand. All day a fierce battle raged with guns, knives, and hatchets. At dusk, the Patriot militia retreated, finally beaten. General Herkimer died of his wounds.

Soon after, an expedition of Continental troops under General Benedict Arnold appeared, and St. Leger retreated. Though British Regulars would never again threaten the Mohawk Valley, Loyalists and Iroquois continued to raid and plunder the region for the rest of the war.

Burgoyne's plan for an invasion from the west had failed. He was alone now, as overwhelming Patriot forces converged on him.

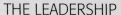

LOYALIST RAIDERS

This brass beltplate was from Butler's Rangers, one of the most feared Loyalist corps. Allied with Indian warriors, they raided farms and settlements along the frontier.

"GR" for "George, Rex" or "King George"

THE LEADERSHIP

COLONEL ST. LEGER HAD SERVED IN THE FRENCH and Indian War and was experienced in wilderness fighting. The Patriot second-in-command at Stanwix, Marinus Willett of New York City, was also a veteran of that war.

"[The Colonel] was determined to defend the fort in favor of the United States to the last extremity."

—Soldier William Colbraith, describing Gansevoort's reply to a surrender demand

PETER GANSEVOORT (1749-1812)

Colonel Gansevoort led the Fort Stanwix garrison that held out against St. Leger's invasion. He was from a prominent Albany family of Dutch descent. Gansevoort received a special commendation from Congress for defending the fort.

"[The rebels] who escaped only served to spread the panic wider."

—St. Leger, expecting victory after Oriskany

JOSEPH BRANT (1742-1807)

Brant's Mohawk name was Thayendanega. Educated in a school for Indians, he had visited England and held an officer's commission in the British army. After the Revolution, he led his people to a new home in Canada.

AN UNIMAGINABLE DEFEAT

In early September, Burgoyne learned that Barry St. Leger's force was retreating to Canada. Even without Howe or St. Leger to join him, Burgoyne still wanted to continue. He gambled that British reinforcements would be sent north from New York. Also, he did not believe that British troops could lose to Americans on the open battlefield.

Burgoyne's army advanced down the Hudson toward Albany. Blocking the way at Saratoga was a Rebel force commanded by General Horatio Gates.

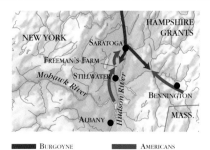

BURGOYNE   AMERICANS

SARATOGA BATTLES
After failing to capture Patriot supplies at Bennington, Burgoyne fought two battles at Freeman's Farm, near the town of Stillwater.

THE LEADERSHIP

BURGOYNE LOST HIS BEST FIELD COMMANDER when Fraser was shot down. No one could take his place. General Gates was ineffective in combat but had excellent commanders, including Benjamin Lincoln, Enoch Poor, and John Glover.

SIMON FRASER (1729-1777)
A gallant Scottish officer and veteran of the French and Indian War, Fraser was greatly admired by both British and American soldiers. After the battle, he was buried on high ground above the Hudson River. During Fraser's funeral, Americans fired cannon in a salute to the fallen enemy officer.

"My duty forbids me to fly from danger."

—Fraser's reply to an aide's warning that he is being targeted

"To Arnold alone is due the honor of our victory."

—Colonel Henry Livingston of the Continental army to Schuyler

BENEDICT ARNOLD (1741-1801)
General Arnold seemed everywhere at once. He marched against St. Leger and led the way at Freeman's Farm. After the campaign, he received the thanks of Congress, but the jealous Gates did not mention him in dispatches.

The British and Americans fought two battles at Freeman's Farm. In the first, on September 19, Burgoyne held the field, but suffered heavy casualties. The second battle, on October 7, was a terrible defeat for the British. Rebel general Benedict Arnold led charge after charge, finally breaking Burgoyne's lines. General Fraser was killed in the fighting. Burgoyne withdrew from the battlefield and regrouped his remaining troops.

Burgoyne's officers advised a retreat to Canada. It was too late; John Stark's militia had cut off the escape route to the north. Burgoyne surrendered his army to Gates on October 17.

Saratoga was a turning point in the Revolution. The capture of Burgoyne's army helped convince the French that the Americans could beat the British. France decided to join the war on the side of the new United States.

The powerful French Navy was essential to the Patriot cause. French warships might intercept British troops and supplies sailing to America. Also, valuable British colonies in the West Indies had to be defended, drawing off thousands of troops from the Revolutionary War.

Blade engraved with coat of arms

GERMAN SPONTOON
Carried by officers as symbols of rank, spontoons could be used as weapons in battle. This one belonged to an officer from the German principality of Brunswick.

FRASER FALLS
Arnold ordered Morgan's riflemen to shoot General Fraser, who was rallying British troops. Perched high in a tree, sharpshooter Timothy Murphy found his target on the third try.

Losses	
American:	140 killed/wounded/missing
British/German:	600 killed/wounded, 5,000 prisoners/missing

PHILADELPHIA FALLS TO HOWE

As General Burgoyne marched southward, Washington was camped with the main Rebel army in New Jersey. The Patriot commander-in-chief was watching Sir William Howe in New York, expecting him to sail up the Hudson River to join Burgoyne.

It was a surprise to Washington when Howe put to sea on July 23, with 260 ships and 15,000 troops. On August 22, the British fleet was sighted in the Chesapeake Bay off the coast of Delaware. Howe was planning to capture Philadelphia, the American capital. Washington hurried south to block Howe's path.

At Brandywine Creek on September 11, Howe attacked Washington. Just as he had at Long Island, Howe made a frontal attack to hold the Americans in position. At the same time, the main British army marched 17 miles (27 kilometers) around the Rebels to strike them from behind. The British crashed against Washington's right, rolling the defenders back. American officers struggled to keep their men together in a fighting retreat.

With the defeat at Brandywine, the Continental Congress fled Philadelphia. The British marched unopposed into the city on September 26. Howe had

UNDER THE GENERAL'S GAZE
Washington assembled a strong army to block Howe's advance on Philadelphia. The Patriot troops were fresh and eager to fight. The British moved fast, however, outflanking the Americans. Though defeated, the Patriot army held together.

Losses	
American:	1,300 killed/wounded/ prisoners/missing
British/German:	577 killed/wounded, 6 prisoners/missing

won another great victory, but again Washington's army had escaped. The Rebels had fought well in retreat and were confident that next time they could win. The capital of the Revolution had fallen, but Howe had not yet won the war.

PHILADELPHIA
British assaults on the front and the right seemed successful until the Americans counterattacked and wiped out the entire enemy force.

■ HOWE'S ATTACK   ■ WASHINGTON

Silver hilt

GRENADIER SWORD
A 19-year-old British grenadier lieutenant killed at Brandywine carried this hunting sword.

THE LEADERSHIP

WASHINGTON HAD A NEW OFFICER IN THE FRENCH Marquis de Lafayette, who joined the Patriot army. Howe's top generals, Knyphausen and Cornwallis, were bold and aggressive in the attack. Major Patrick Ferguson, later killed at King's Mountain, also led troops for Howe.

JOHN SULLIVAN (1740-1795)
Washington considered General Sullivan, a New Hampshireman, one of his most dependable generals. At Brandywine, Sullivan's division was forced to retreat. Some blamed him for the defeat, but Washington did not. In 1779, Sullivan led an expedition that defeated Iroquois Loyalists. This stopped much of the frontier raiding.

"Your duty as a general was not well performed."
—Member of Congress Thomas Burke of North Carolina, criticizing Sullivan

WILLIAM HOWE (1729-1814)
Capturing the Rebel capital seemed a great victory at first. Howe was faulted, however, for not wiping out the Patriot army. Despite his triumphs he would soon be replaced by his subordinate Sir Henry Clinton.

"Philadelphia has captured Howe."
—Benjamin Franklin, meaning the general was out of the war in Philadelphia

A VICTORY SLIPS AWAY

In October, 9,000 of Howe's Regulars were camped at Germantown, five miles (8 kilometers) north of Philadelphia. Washington planned a surprise attack with 11,000 Continentals and militia. Dividing his army into columns, Washington marched them through the night. Early morning fog hid the attackers, and the assault was a complete surprise to the British.

The center Patriot column, under General John Sullivan, smashed deep into enemy lines. British Lieutenant Colonel Thomas Musgrave sent 120 Regulars into the stone mansion of Loyalist Benjamin Chew. Instead of bypassing it, the Americans tried to capture the house. The Regulars held out fiercely, and the Rebel attack lost momentum. Sullivan's advance stalled at the Chew House.

Patriot troops under General Nathanael Greene swung out wide to attack the British right. The maneuver took too long. By the time Greene finally hit the British, Sullivan's men were running out of ammunition.

Then, in the thick fog, American troops accidentally fired on one another, causing panic. Seeing the Rebel advance had slowed,

STORMING THE CHEW HOUSE
Washington ordered an assault on the stone house. He did not want to leave an enemy strongpoint behind his army. The 120 British inside held on, and more than 50 Americans lay dying on the lawns after the failed attack.

Top

SOLDIER'S CANTEEN
British and American troops used tin canteens. They were carried on straps slung over the shoulders or fixed to belts.

Strap

Losses		
American:	152 killed, 521 wounded, 400 prisoners/missing	
British/German:	537 killed/wounded, 14 prisoners/missing	

the Regulars counterattacked furiously. Washington had to call a retreat. The British, still recovering from their surprise, did not try to follow.

The Continental Army had recovered well after Brandywine, and came close to winning a victory at Germantown. As they went into winter quarters at Valley Forge, the Patriots were eager to fight again in the coming spring. Yet, they needed training. That winter, former Prussian drillmaster Friedrich von Steuben appeared and transformed Washington's army.

HOWE   WASHINGTON'S ATTACK

A DIFFICULT PLAN

The Patriots were to advance in four columns at night and attack at the same time. This was difficult for troops who were not thoroughly trained. Fog contributed to the confusion, and the army could not carry out the plan.

THE LEADERSHIP

GENERAL HOWE WON THE FIELD but lost valuable officers: British general James Agnew was killed, and several colonels were killed or wounded. Patriot general Peter Muhlenberg, a Lutheran clergyman, drove deep into enemy lines with his brigade. He was surrounded but fought his way out.

"We ought to have pushed our advantage, leaving a party to watch the enemy in that house."

—from the journal of Timothy Pickering

TIMOTHY PICKERING (1745–1829)

Colonel Pickering was a Patriot staff officer. The army used a training manual he had written for Massachusetts militia. Pickering objected to attacking the Chew House. He later became an effective quartermaster general in charge of supplying the army.

"All retreated to Germantown except Colonel Musgrave, who ... nobly defended [the] house till we were reinforced ..."

—British Lieutenant Sir Martin Hunter, diary entry

THOMAS MUSGRAVE (1737–1812)

Lieutenant Colonel Musgrave commanded the 40th Regiment of Foot at Germantown. He counterattacked the Americans and slowed their advance. Next, he gathered 120 men in the Chew House. A storm of bullets and cannonballs hit the house, but Musgrave refused to surrender.

France Renews Hope for the Patriots

The British spent the winter in Philadelphia. The loss of the city was a heavy blow to Congress, which now governed from York, Pennsylvania. Washington's army camped at nearby Valley Forge.

At first, many of Washington's soldiers had no clothes or shoes, and food was scarce. To improve conditions, Nathanael Greene took charge of supplying the army. Greene did his job well, and life became better for the men. The Prussian officer Baron Friedrich von Steuben arrived at Valley Forge as a volunteer. He began drilling the soldiers in strict European battle tactics and how to use the bayonet.

By February, the joyful news came that France had made an alliance with the United States. This worried British leaders, who were also unhappy that Howe had not destroyed Washington's army. The British were on the defensive now that France had entered

FRONTIER WARFARE
George Rogers Clark's expedition captures British-held Fort Sackville in the Illinois country. Clark broke the British grip on what was then known as the Northwest.

VALLEY FORGE
General Washington meets a sentry in the encampment at Valley Forge. The winter of 1777–1778 was often a hungry one, but the army drilled hard and by spring was ready for battle.

February	May	June	July
Treaty of Alliance signed by France and the United States	Clinton replaces Howe as Commander of British forces in America	Battle of Monmouth	Loyalists, Indians massacre settlers in Wyoming Valley, Pennsylvania
Von Steuben starts training at Valley Forge		George Rogers Clark begins his campaign	France declares war on Britain

the war. General Sir Henry Clinton replaced Howe and was ordered to withdraw to New York.

As Clinton marched across New Jersey, Washington attacked him at Monmouth Courthouse on June 28. This last great battle in the North was a draw. Clinton marched on to New York, and Washington followed close behind.

On the western frontier, Virginia Patriot George Rogers Clark led an expedition of tough Kentucky riflemen. On July 4, Clark took British fort Kaskaskia, and soon after, Vincennes. Now, the only royal authority on the frontier was at Fort Detroit and to the north at Fort Michilimackinac.

FRANKLIN IN PARIS

Britain and France had been at peace since 1763, when the British won the Seven Years' War. In 1778, the French saw a chance to defeat Britain by aiding the Americans. Patriot military achievements had proven the Revolutionaries were determined to achieve independence. Benjamin Franklin was then in France representing Congress. His fame as a scientist and writer made him welcome at the French court. Franklin's skillful diplomacy influenced the decision of King Louis XVI to back the American Revolution.

THE DIPLOMAT AND THE KING
Benjamin Franklin bows to King Louis XVI. Franklin's diplomacy helped win France as an ally.

August	September	November	December
French and American forces fail in their siege of British-held Newport, Rhode Island	Shawnee lay siege to Boonesboro, Kentucky, but defenders hold out	Loyalists and Indians strike settlers in Cherry Valley, New York	Savannah, Georgia falls to the British

A HARD-FOUGHT DRAW

In the spring of 1778, General Clinton prepared to evacuate Philadelphia and return to New York. With France in the war, many of Clinton's soldiers were needed to defend other parts of the British Empire. On June 16, his army marched out of Philadelphia in a long column of 10,000 men, heading for Sandy Hook, New Jersey. From there British ships would ferry the army to New York.

On June 28, in sweltering 100-degree (38-degree-Celsius) heat, Washington's army attacked Clinton's rear guard at Monmouth, New Jersey. The Patriot offensive succeeded at first. Then Clinton made an aggressive counterattack. Washington's second-in-command, General Charles Lee, ordered a retreat. Lee did not believe the Continentals were a match for British Regulars.

Washington was furious to see the army falling back. Taking over command, he ordered Lee to the rear. A new defensive line was formed, and the Patriots repelled one British charge after another. Washington did not have enough fresh soldiers to make a decisive counterattack.

The terrible heat exhausted both armies, and the Battle of Monmouth was a hard-fought draw. In the cool of

WASHINGTON SCOLDS LEE
While riding to join the battle, Washington meets General Lee, in retreat. Furious, Washington ordered Lee to the rear and took command himself, stopping the retreat and reforming the army.

Losses	
American:	72 killed, 161 wounded, 132 prisoners/missing
British:	358 killed/wounded, 600 prisoners/missing

the night, Clinton's army marched away to Sandy Hook, then sailed to New York. Washington followed and set up camp near the city in White Plains. Monmouth was the last great battle in the North.

FUSILIER SWORD

This sword is from the famed Royal Welsh Fusiliers (23rd Regiment), which fought in almost every major engagement from Concord to Yorktown. The grip bears the regimental device.

ATTACKING THE REAR GUARD

Washington planned to strike at the British rear guard as Clinton's column marched across New Jersey. A full-scale battle began when Clinton turned to fight.

CLINTON   WASHINGTON

THE LEADERSHIP

GENERAL LEE RETURNED TO WASHINGTON'S ARMY after more than a year as a prisoner. Lee did not believe the Patriots could outfight the British. Clinton had commanders Cornwallis and Colonel Henry Monckton in the action.

HENRY CLINTON (1730-1795)

General Clinton relieved Howe in May and was ordered to withdraw to New York. Clinton was the son of a former New York governor and had grown up in the colony. He was commander-in-chief, headquartered in New York City, until 1782.

"[You face] a situation which, I fear, you will not find a bed of roses."

—Cornwallis to Clinton, just named commander-in-chief

CHARLES LEE (1731-1782)

A former British officer, Lee believed he should be in command, not Washington. He had been a soldier of fortune who also fought for Poland. Lee was court-martialed after Monmouth and did not return to the army.

"Sir, you do not know British soldiers. We cannot stand against them."

—Lee, at Monmouth, telling Lafayette they must retreat

CLARK'S GRUELING MARCH

In June 1778, frontier leader George Rogers Clark set out to attack key British outposts. These posts were supplying hostile Indian warriors with rum, guns, and gunpowder. Clark led 200 Kentucky riflemen who were known as "Longknives" because they carried large hunting knives. Clark captured the post at Kaskaskia and Fort Sackville at Vincennes without a shot.

Most Indian tribes in the region stayed neutral. They respected Clark's courage and trusted his promises of peace. In Fort Detroit to the north, British Colonel Henry Hamilton knew he must counter Clark's invasion. Hamilton marched out with a force of mostly Loyalist militia and Indians. On December 17, he recaptured Fort Sackville. Clark had left only a few men to defend the fort.

Clark soon gathered his Longknives at Kaskaskia and set out on a 180-mile (290-kilometer) march to attack Hamilton. It was mid-February, and the frozen waterways and swamps near Vincennes were flooded. The Kentuckians slogged through waist-deep icy water. Clark's arrival at Vincennes surprised Hamilton, who prepared to defend the post. Clark marched his riflemen back and forth in the woods outside the fort, beating drums and waving battle flags. Hamilton was tricked into thinking the Americans far outnumbered him. He surrendered on February 24.

Clark had won a great victory, but in the years to come bitter war between whites and Indians continued along the American frontier.

THROUGH SPRING FLOODS
Clark leads his expedition into icy Wabash River floods to attack Vincennes. This ordeal gave the Kentuckians the element of surprise. Hamilton expected a strike, but not while the country was flooded.

Losses	
American:	negligible
British:	115 prisoners

VIRGINIA SWORD
Though not the long knife that earned Kentuckians their nickname, this French-made sword was issued by Virginia to one of Clark's frontiersmen.

Blade is inscribed "Grenadier of Virginia" and "Victory or Death"

CLARK'S JOURNEYS
In the campaign's first phase, Clark won frontier posts with no bloodshed. After Hamilton retook Fort Sackville, which defended Vincennes, Clark returned to lay siege to the fort.

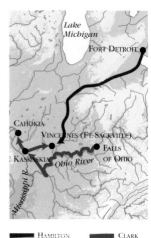

HAMILTON ▬▬▬ CLARK

THE LEADERSHIP

GEORGE ROGERS CLARK INSPIRED HIS MEN with his courage and endurance. He won over local French leaders such as Père Gibault who kept their people neutral. Henry Hamilton, however, lacked French support.

GEORGE ROGERS CLARK (1752–1818)
Colonel Clark's exploits won him the title, "Conqueror of the Old Northwest"—the region south of the Great Lakes. A surveyor, explorer, and militia captain, he had fought in Indian conflicts before the Revolution.

"Our suffering for four days in crossing those waters...[was] too incredible to believe."
—Clark to friend George Mason

HENRY HAMILTON (d. 1796)
Commander of Fort Detroit, Colonel Hamilton had served in the French and Indian War. In the Revolution, he sent Loyalist white and Indian raiders against frontier settlements. He was falsely accused of buying scalps taken from slain Patriots.

"The English to a man declared they would stand to the last...[but to depend on] the French was to depend on traitors."
—Hamilton, saying the local militia would not fight Clark

The War Goes South, Lost Battles

The American Revolution widened to become a world war. France's ally, Spain, declared war on Britain in 1779. The Netherlands also entered the war on the American side.

The European empires fought for control of colonies around the world. At sea, John Paul Jones raided the coast of Britain and sank a Royal Navy ship in a fight to the finish.

The British moved the war South, capturing Savannah by early 1779. In the North there was a stalemate between Sir Henry Clinton, who was defending New York, and Washington, who was besieging it. That October, French and American troops were defeated trying to retake Savannah.

In May 1780, Clinton captured Charleston, South Carolina, and the

A BOLD CAPTAIN
John Paul Jones took the former merchant ship *Bonhomme Richard* into battle against stiff odds in September 1779. Jones attacked the British Navy's *Serapis,* though he had fewer guns. Jones captured the *Serapis,* but his own ship soon sank.

June 1778	July 1778	September 1778	October 1782
Spain declares war on Britain	Battle of Stony Point	*Bonhomme Richard* sinks HMS *Serapis*	Siege of Savannah Washington sets up winter quarters at Morristown, New Jersey

7,000 Americans defending it. The Patriots suffered another blow this year when General Benedict Arnold proved to be a traitor. Arnold tried to surrender West Point to the British, but the plot failed. He narrowly escaped and joined the British army.

Congress appointed General Horatio Gates to stop the British invasion of the South. But in August 1780, Gates's army was destroyed at Camden, South Carolina. Still, the Southern militia kept up the fight. In October, Patriots wiped out a strong Loyalist force at King's Mountain, South Carolina.

That December, Washington sent his best general, Nathanael Greene, to gather the scattered rebel forces and win back the South.

TAKING COMMAND
Nathanael Greene, left, salutes Horatio Gates as Greene arrives to rebuild the southern Patriot army. Greene faced a superior enemy force, but he kept the Revolution alive in the South. Gates became an administrative officer.

ARNOLD'S BETRAYAL

Patriots were shocked when the hero of Saratoga went over to the enemy. In mid-1779, Benedict Arnold plotted to let the British take West Point, which he commanded. Arnold was angry with Congress. He believed its members had not treated him fairly. The British promised him a large reward for joining them. The plot was discovered, and Arnold escaped. He later became a general in the king's service and fought the Patriots.

CAPTURING A SPY
British officer John André was disguised as a civilian. His arrest revealed Benedict Arnold's plot to surrender West Point.

May 1779	July 1779	August 1779	October 1779
British capture Charleston, South Carolina	5,000 French troops under General Rochambeau arrive at Newport, Rhode Island	Gates's army is destroyed by Cornwallis at Camden, South Carolina	Battle of King's Mountain, South Carolina
			General Nathanael Greene replaces Gates

NIGHT ATTACK, BY BAYONET

The fortress of West Point guarded the Hudson River 50 miles (80 kilometers) above New York. West Point protected Patriot supplies and troops as they were ferried across the

"Carry me up to the fort, boys!"

—Bleeding from a scalp wound, Wayne orders his men forward

river. In early June, General Clinton sailed up the Hudson and took a fort at Stony Point. Clinton now threatened West Point itself.

Washington ordered General Anthony Wayne to recapture Stony Point. On July 15, Wayne's 1,300-man force marched through the darkness and attacked. In a surprise midnight

SURPRISE ATTACK
Wayne advanced secretly toward Stony Point. After dark, his force assembled in silence close to the fort, then attacked.

CLINTON
WAYNE

assault, the Americans used only bayonets. They captured the fort after a brief, fierce struggle. This success helped protect West Point and also lifted Patriot spirits. Even the British admired the brave, skillful assault. American soldiers had come far since 1775.

THE LEADERSHIP

FRENCH OFFICER COLONEL TEISSEDRE DE FLEURY led one assault and tore down the enemy flag. British commander, Colonel Henry Johnson, continued to serve in the war.

STORMING A FORTRESS
The British were famous for unstoppable bayonet charges. At Stony Point the Americans won a reputation of their own for bayonet attacks. The Patriots had benefited from the strict training of Baron von Steuben.

ANTHONY WAYNE (1745–1796)
A Pennsylvanian, General Wayne's daring in battle earned the nickname "Mad Anthony." He fought from the early Canadian invasion to the final Southern campaigns in 1783.

Losses	
American:	15 killed, 83 wounded
British:	20 killed, 74 wounded, 530 prisoners/missing

JONES SPURNS DEFEAT

The British Navy ruled the seas. The Patriot navy was small, so Congress gave privately owned civilian ships permission to attack the enemy. These "privateers" sank or captured thousands of British vessels.

The most successful privateer was Commodore John Paul Jones. Based in France, Jones raided British coastal villages and captured cargo ships and fishing boats. His squadron of vessels was led by his flagship, *Bonhomme Richard*. On September 23, Jones attacked a British convoy guarded by the warship HMS *Serapis*. Jones's crew lashed the ships together with ropes. This forced a close-range struggle with muskets, swords, and hand-grenades.

The battle raged by moonlight until the *Serapis* lowered her flag and surrendered to Jones.

"I have not yet begun to fight!"
—Jones, when Pearson asked if he was giving up

AROUND BRITAIN
Setting out from French naval base L'Orient, Jones captured vessels and raided seaports all along the coast of Britain.

▬▬ JONES

THE LEADERSHIP

CAPTAIN JONES HAD INEXPERIENCED OFFICERS on his vessel. The British, under Captain Richard Pearson, were naval men. American Lieutenant Richard Dale recorded Jones's answer to Pearson.

NAVAL HAND GRENADE

JOHN PAUL JONES (1747–1792)
Scottish-born Jones came to America just before the war. He joined the new Continental Navy, and his many wartime triumphs won him fame. The American navy was disbanded after the war, and Jones later fought for Russia against the Turks.

HURLING DEFIANCE
His vessel shot full of holes and leaking, Jones shouts through a speaking trumpet, refusing to surrender. Half his 237-man crew were casualties after the hand-to-hand battle.

Losses	
American:	120 killed/wounded
British:	117 killed/wounded

DEFEAT AT SAVANNAH

War had come to the southern colonies in December 1778 when the British captured the port city of Savannah, Georgia. Soon all the state was under British control. Instead of 13 colonies in rebellion, there were now 12.

General Benjamin Lincoln was commander of the Continental forces in the region. In September 1779, Lincoln combined with a French fleet and soldiers under Admiral Comte d'Estaing to attack Savannah. Lincoln marched his army toward the city as 33 French warships appeared in the harbor.

D'Estaing landed 4,000 French soldiers and demanded the city's surrender. Lincoln soon arrived with the American army, bringing the siege force to 6,500 men. Though British general Augustine

Regimental symbol

FRENCH BADGE
A French infantryman in the Regiment de Foix at Savannah had this brass badge on his cartridge box.

THE LEADERSHIP

AT SAVANNAH, COUNT D'ESTAING did not cooperate with the Americans. General Benjamin Lincoln objected when D'Estaing demanded the British surrender to "the arms of the King of France."

AUGUSTINE PREVOST (1723-1786)
General Prevost had been an officer in the 60th Foot (Royal American Regiment) during the French and Indian War. After defending Savannah, he left for England, closing a career of 22 years in North America and the Caribbean.

"[This is] the greatest event that has happened in the whole war."

—General Clinton, praising Prevost's victory

COUNT CHARLES D'ESTAING (1729-1794)
This French admiral had also served as an army officer when a young man. D'Estaing was unsuccessful as an admiral, with several failures during the American Revolution. Respected for his courage, he was wounded leading an assault on Savannah.

"Our situation had become terrible and disheartening."

—A French officer, after a failed attack

Prevost had only 2,400 defenders, he was determined to hold out.

The siege went too slowly for the French. D'Estaing had only a short time before the hurricane season arrived. He needed to return to safe harbors in the Caribbean. On October 9, D'Estaing and Lincoln launched a frontal assault on Prevost's defenses, which proved too strong. Americans and French were mowed down by musket and cannon fire, and the attack was shattered. D'Estaing was dismayed by the repulse. With no more time to spare, he broke off the siege and sailed away. Without the French, Lincoln withdrew to Charleston, leaving Georgia firmly in British hands.

LAND AND SEA CAMPAIGN
Lincoln moved his army from Charleston to Savannah while D'Estaing's French fleet sailed from the West Indies.

■ AMERICAN AND FRENCH FORCES

Losses

American/French:	203 killed, 600 wounded/ prisoners/missing
British:	16 killed, 39 wounded

FALL OF A BRAVE OFFICER
Polish count Casimir Pulaski was killed at Savannah. He died leading a reckless cavalry charge against waiting infantry. Pulaski's career was marked by frequent conflict with American officers and by several defeats.

LINCOLN LOSES AN ARMY

After taking Georgia, Clinton moved against Charleston, South Carolina. General Benjamin Lincoln commanded the Patriots defending

> *"Cannon balls whizzing and... ammunition chests blowing up... wounded men groaning... It was a dreadful night."*

—Lincoln, describing the last day of the siege

CHARLESTON BESIEGED
After failure at Savannah, Lincoln retreated to Charleston. Clinton moved against Charleston in spring of 1780.

▨ CLINTON
▧ LINCOLN

the city. In February, the British began a siege. Lincoln did his best to resist, but Clinton's lines moved closer each day. In April, British cavalry leader Banastre Tarleton won a key battle to close the last route to the city. Soon, British cannon were firing into Charleston. To prevent more loss of life and destruction, Lincoln had to surrender. Clinton captured 5,500 troops and piles of military stores. The loss of Charleston and Lincoln's army was a heavy blow to the Revolution.

THE LEADERSHIP

LINCOLN'S GENERALS INCLUDED NORTH CAROLINA'S James Hogun, Virginia's William Woodford, and South Carolina's William Moultrie. Clinton's operations were aided by the able Royal Navy lieutenant, George Elphinstone.

BENJAMIN LINCOLN (1733–1810)
General Lincoln, of Massachusetts, was one of the most solid Patriot leaders. A fine organizer, he served in major campaigns, including Boston, New York, Philadelphia, Saratoga, and Yorktown.

SOUTH CAROLINA REGIMENTAL BUTTON

CITY UNDER BOMBARDMENT
A view of Charleston from British lines, during the 1780 siege, shows artillery shells hitting the city, sending up plumes of smoke.

Losses	
American:	92 killed, 140 wounded, 5,500 prisoners/missing
British:	268 killed/wounded

GATES IS ROUTED

In July, Congress sent Horatio Gates to take command of the scattered Patriot forces in North Carolina. As the victor of Saratoga, Gates was considered a brilliant general. He had 3,000 troops, but mistakenly believed

> *"For God's sake...*
> *send Greene!"*
>
> —Alexander Hamilton, hearing about the defeat

he had 7,000. He went after British general Cornwallis, commanding 2,000 veteran Regulars and Loyalists. Ignoring advice from his officers, Gates marched his men too far and too fast. His soldiers grew weak from fatigue and hunger. Cornwallis attacked Gates at Camden on August 16.

ADVANCE AND RETREAT Shown are British and American marches to Camden, and the escape north of the routed American forces.

▬▬ CORNWALLIS

▬▬ GATES

Cornwallis's soldiers tore through Gates's weary army, completely routing it. Even before the battle had ended, Gates jumped on a horse and galloped away. His reputation was ruined, and the Carolinas lay at Cornwallis's feet.

THE LEADERSHIP

GATES HAD TOP OFFICERS, including generals William Smallwood and Mordecai Gist of Maryland. Cornwallis had the experienced colonel, Lord Francis Rawdon.

FRANCIS RAWDON HASTINGS (1754–1826)
Lord Rawdon's steady leadership helped bring victory at Camden. The colonel was only in his mid-twenties. He had fought at Breed's Hill and served as aide to Clinton and Cornwallis. He went on to be governor general of India.

DEATH OF GENERAL DE KALB
A last stand by Patriots under General Johann de Kalb ended with his death from 11 wounds. De Kalb had come to America with Lafayette and was devoted to the Patriot cause. Gates ignored De Kalb's warning that the Southern army was not prepared to fight Cornwallis.

Losses

American:	1,000 killed, 1,000 wounded, 2,300 prisoners/missing
British:	68 killed, 256 wounded

PATRIOTS DEFEAT LOYALISTS

With the defeats at Charleston and Camden, many Carolinians openly declared themselves Loyalists. Cornwallis sent Lieutenant Colonel Patrick Ferguson to organize them. Ferguson warned the Patriots to surrender or be attacked.

In September, Patriot backwoodsmen from North Carolina, western Virginia, and South Carolina united to oppose Ferguson. On October 7, 900 Patriots led by backwoods colonel Isaac Shelby attacked Ferguson's 900 Loyalists. Two armies of Americans were fighting each other, as in a civil war.

Shelby's force surrounded Ferguson, who defended King's Mountain, South Carolina. The Patriots swarmed up the steep, rocky slopes and fired from behind trees and boulders. They shot down Loyalists with deadly accuracy. Ferguson himself was picked off as he tried to rally his men. When the Loyalists raised the white flag, the Patriots kept shooting them. Shelby finally stopped the firing, barely avoiding a massacre. This battle proved how deep the hatred often was between Patriot and Loyalist.

THE LEADERSHIP

COLONELS ISAAC SHELBY, JOHN SEVIER, and Benjamin Cleveland were key Patriot leaders. Ferguson's subordinates included ranger captain Abraham de Peyster, a New York Loyalist.

ISAAC SHELBY (1750–1826)

A North Carolina militia leader, Colonel Shelby was experienced in wilderness campaigning. Shelby planned the attack at King's Mountain. He later moved to Kentucky and became that state's first governor.

"Shout like hell and fight like the devil!"

—Shelby to his men at the height of battle

PATRICK FERGUSON (1744–1780)

Major Ferguson was a skilled ranger and a marksman with the rifle. A Scot, he was a career army officer. He invented a breech-loading rifle that was faster to load than muzzle-loaders. He made samples for the army, but after Ferguson's death Howe lost interest in breech-loaders.

"[I shall] never yield to such ... banditti!"

—Ferguson, just before he was shot down

The defeat at King's Mountain cost Cornwallis an important part of his army. He had counted on a rising of Loyalists in the South. With the Patriots in power, most Loyalist sympathizers would have to remain quiet. Cornwallis was forced to withdraw to South Carolina to reorganize his force.

At this time, Washington ordered General Nathanael Greene to replace Gates. At crucial moments, Washington often depended on Greene, who was a fine strategist. Greene hurried southward to take command of the shattered Patriot forces. The war in the South had reached a critical and dangerous stage for the Revolution.

FERGUSON ─────── MILITIA

KING'S MOUNTAIN
Ferguson's Loyalists turned south, pursued by a force of back country riflemen, who caught up at King's Mountain. Many of the backwoods militia had come from over the Blue Ridge Mountains.

Strap

Metal lid

ELEGANT POWDER HORN
Some powder horns were fitted with cast metal lids that sealed tightly. The lids often were hinged for easy opening.

FERGUSON FALLS
As his men died all around him, Major Ferguson led a desperate counterattack. He charged and slashed with his sword until several bullets brought him down.

Losses	
Patriot:	28 killed, 64 wounded
Loyalist:	157 killed, 861 wounded/ prisoners

Washington Closes the Ring

War raged throughout British America in 1781. Washington kept up the siege of New York, and Nathanael Greene opened a new campaign to hold the Southern states.

Meanwhile, the French and Spanish battled the British for control of valuable Caribbean Islands. Early in the year, British West Florida fell to the Spanish.

In January, Daniel Morgan destroyed a British force at The Cowpens, South Carolina. In March, Cornwallis defeated Greene at Guilford Court House, North Carolina. Cornwallis lost many more men than Greene, whose army escaped. Cornwallis next marched into Virginia, trying to defeat Lafayette's army. Cornwallis could not catch Lafayette and instead went to Yorktown for reinforcements. In August, a French fleet sailed toward Chesapeake Bay to

SWORDS AND PISTOLS
An African-American bodyservant and trumpeter, left, saves his officer's life at the Battle of The Cowpens by shooting at British dragoons, right. This incident occurred at The Cowpens early in 1781.

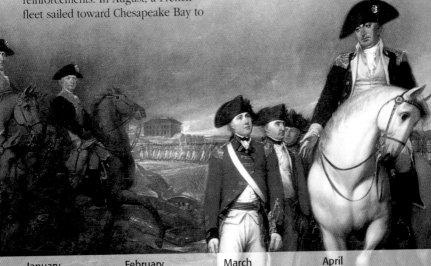

January	February	March	April
Mutiny of the Pennsylvania Line	Lafayette begins his Virginia Campaign	Battle of Guilford Court House, North Carolina	Battle of Hobkirk's Hill, South Carolina
Battle of The Cowpens, South Carolina			

blockade Yorktown. Seeing a chance to trap Cornwallis, Washington and French commander Rochambeau hurried their armies southward. Soon, Cornwallis was surrounded.

That September, Greene was driven from the battlefield at Eutaw Springs, South Carolina, but the British lost so heavily that they withdrew to Charleston.

Besieged at Yorktown, Cornwallis surrendered on October 19. The Siege of Yorktown was the last great battle of the American Revolution. By now, British troops were pinned in the seaport cities of New York, Charleston, and Savannah.

CONTINENTAL $5 BILL

MUTINY OF THE LINE

Many Patriot soldiers were disgusted at lack of pay or supplies from Congress. In January 1781, several hundred Pennsylvania troops marched toward Philadelphia to demand better treatment. At the last moment, General Anthony Wayne convinced them not to threaten Congress. When Congress agreed not to punish them, they ended their mutiny. Other regiments soon followed with their own mutinies. New Jersey mutineers were arrested and their leaders executed by firing squads.

WASHINGTON'S TRIUMPH
American second-in-command General Benjamin Lincoln, mounted, accepts the surrender of the British army at Yorktown. Commander-in-chief George Washington, center right, looks on.

CHALLENGING WAYNE
Mutineers confront Anthony Wayne as he arrives at their camp; Wayne persuaded them to return to their regiments.

May	June	September	October
Pensacola, Florida falls to Spain	Rawdon lifts the Patriot siege of Ft. Ninety-Six, South Carolina	Battle of the Virginia (Chesapeake) Capes	Cornwallis surrenders at Yorktown, Virginia
		Battle of Eutaw Springs, South Carolina	

MORGAN WHIPS TARLETON

In January 1781, Greene detached Daniel Morgan with 1,000 men to threaten the British supply line. Cornwallis sent Tarleton and 1,100 crack troops after Morgan, who made a stand in South Carolina. The field of battle was a cattle pasture known as The Cowpens.

At dawn on January 17, Tarleton's regiments rushed across the meadow toward Morgan's front ranks—militia from the Carolinas and Georgia. Following Morgan's plan, the militia fired a volley and withdrew. Next the British met Morgan's main body, mostly seasoned Continentals from Delaware and Maryland. Their fire stopped the attackers. Because of a misunderstanding, the Continentals then withdrew, but in good order. At this crucial moment, Morgan rode up and told them to reform. The enemy attackers ran into a devastating volley from the reorganized Continentals, who counterattacked with the bayonet. The

shattered Redcoats were overwhelmed, forced to surrender or die.

Meanwhile, Tarleton's 50 dragoons had galloped through the American left, sabers slashing. They were counterattacked by 150 Continental dragoons. The British cavalry was cut to pieces. The Battle of The Cowpens lasted only an hour, but Tarleton's force was badly mauled. Only he and about 175 others escaped.

The victory raised Patriot spirits in the South, and militia began to muster for Greene. The battle proved that brave militia troops under excellent leadership could defeat the best Regulars. The Continental dragoons, led by Virginia Colonel William

PATRIOT DRAGOONS ATTACK
Virginia colonel William Washington leads his troopers in a charge that scattered Tarleton's dragoons. This clash sealed the American victory at The Cowpens and the destruction of Tarleton's army.

Losses	
American:	12 killed, 60 wounded
British:	100 killed, 829 wounded/ prisoners

Washington, especially distinguished themselves in the battle.

Cornwallis once again lost the advantage to the Patriots in the South. He also had lost a large part of his army and was in desperate need of reinforcements.

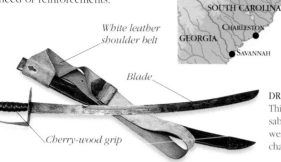

■■■ TARLETON
■■■ MORGAN

White leather shoulder belt

Blade

Cherry-wood grip

DRAGOON SABER
This American cavalryman's saber was a fearsome weapon in the hands of a charging horseman.

THE LEADERSHIP

BANASTRE TARLETON'S OFFENSIVE STYLE of battle was no match for Daniel Morgan's cool-headed defensive tactics. Both had excellent subordinate commanders.

"Our success must be attributed to the justice of our cause and the bravery of our troops."

—General Daniel Morgan

DANIEL MORGAN (1736–1802)
A brilliant leader of Virginia riflemen, Morgan had retired from the American service in 1779, but returned in 1780 to serve against Cornwallis. Morgan was highly regarded for his courage and skill while personally leading troops in battle, especially at the momentous American victory at Saratoga in 1777.

"When I advance, I must either destroy Morgan's corps or push it before me over Broad River...."

—Colonel Banastre Tarleton

BANASTRE TARLETON (1754–1833)
Tarleton was a hardhitting young British cavalry officer. He was blamed for a massacre of American prisoners by his troops, after the Americans had surrendered. As leader of the Loyalist force, the British Legion, he was considered an up-and-coming field commander until being humiliated by the loss of his entire command at The Cowpens.

A STEP AHEAD OF DEFEAT

In January of 1781, turncoat Benedict Arnold joined Colonel John Simcoe to raid and burn Patriot communities throughout Virginia. Virginia had given the Continental army some of its best troops. Now these men were with Washington to the north, or with Greene to the south fighting for the Carolinas.

To protect Virginia—his own home state—Washington sent French volunteer Marquis de Lafayette southward with 1,200 Continental troops. Though just 23 years old, Lafayette was a fine leader.

Lafayette was outnumbered, but he harassed Arnold and Simcoe and kept them from taking control of the region. In May, Cornwallis brought his own army north to Virginia and took command of royal forces there. Lafayette had to keep his troops from being caught by this fast-moving British general. The young French nobleman skillfully stayed a step ahead

YOUTHFUL GENERAL
The Marquis de Lafayette was 19 in 1777, when he volunteered for the Revolution. His wealth and influence convinced Congress to make him a general immediately. He later helped persuade France to become an ally.

"USA" BELT PLATE
Lafayette issued French-made brass belt plates to noncommissioned officers in the infantry corps he led. The belt plate bore the letters "USA" in honor of the new nation.

Losses	
American:	37 killed, 113 wounded, 26 prisoners/missing
British:	108 killed/wounded/ prisoners/missing

of Cornwallis, taking every chance to turn and fight.

On July 6, Cornwallis lured Lafayette into a trap. At Green Spring, Virginia, Cornwallis pretended to cross the James River. Instead, he sent only a few troops to the other side, keeping most of his army ready. Lafayette took the bait, thinking he would catch Cornwallis's army divided by the river. Lafayette attacked, but at the last moment he sensed a trap. He pulled back most of his troops and withdrew just in time to save his army.

THE VIRGINIA CAMPAIGN
With a small force, Lafayette harassed the British in Virginia until Cornwallis went to Yorktown. Then Lafayette closed in to await Washington's army.

■■■ CORNWALLIS   ■■■ LAFAYETTE

THE LEADERSHIP

LAFAYETTE COOPERATED WITH GENERALS Anthony Wayne and Baron von Steuben. Opposed were top British generals Benedict Arnold, John Simcoe, their commander William Phillips, and later Burgoyne.

MARQUIS DE LAFAYETTE (1757–1834)
French nobleman Marie Joseph du Motier, the Marquis de Lafayette, admired American liberty. Though inexperienced at soldiering, Lafayette had natural ability as a commander. He spent much of his personal fortune in support of the Revolution.

"I am not strong enough even to get beaten."

—Lafayette, whose army was too weak to stand and fight

JOHN GRAVES SIMCOE (1752–1806)
A British officer, Colonel Simcoe led the Loyalist Queen's Rangers. They captured Stony Point in 1779. He defeated Patriot militias in the Virginia campaign before surrendering with Burgoyne at Yorktown.

"[Some rebel militia] were deceived by the dress of the Rangers [and] came to Lt. Col. Simcoe, who . . . sent them [as] prisoners to General Arnold."

—Simcoe's memoir, describing his capture of confused Patriots

SPANISH SEIZE WEST FLORIDA

Spain owned Louisiana, including the city of New Orleans. Bernardo de Galvez, the colony's governor, had secretly supplied the American rebels with guns, powder, and cash. When war broke out between Spain and Britain in 1779, Galvez attacked from New Orleans. His troops captured British outposts along the Mississippi and took control of the southern portion of the river.

In 1780, Galvez began a campaign against the British colonies of East and West Florida. (West Florida included part of what became Alabama.) Galvez captured the key British port of Mobile. Pensacola, the center of British power in West Florida, still held out.

During the winter of 1781, Galvez organized a powerful invasion force. On March 9, the Spanish fleet arrived off Pensacola, and Galvez's 8,000 troops surrounded the British stronghold. Though he had only 1,900 men, 900 of them Regulars, British general John Campbell refused to surrender. A siege continued until May 8, when Spanish gunners hit a powder magazine. This set off a deadly explosion. A hundred British defenders

THE LEADERSHIP

BRITAIN HAD FEW OFFICERS TO SPARE for West Florida, so Campbell had little support. Galvez had 10,000 available troops, their commanders, and the Spanish navy with him.

BERNARDO DE GALVEZ (1746–1786)
Governor de Galvez had experience as a commander in Spanish colonial wars. Between 1779–1781, Galvez took every British fort in West Florida. He later was promoted to become the Viceroy of Mexico.

"[The Spanish wanted] the navigation of the Mississippi as consideration for aid. [I told them] that God Almighty had made that river a highway for [Americans]."

—Diplomat John Jay bargains for Spanish financial support

JOHN CAMPBELL (d. 1806)
General Campbell was an officer in the Black Watch Highlanders and fought in the French and Indian War. After serving at New York City, he took command in West Florida. He was ordered to capture New Orleans, but did not have the force to do so.

"[They] sacrificed to their fury all whom they found."

—Spanish officer's report on a British-Indian raid on the Mississippi in 1780

were killed in the blast. Galvez attacked immediately, but Campbell drove the Spanish back. A second assault took a section of Pensacola's fortifications. From there the Spanish could fire directly into the fort. Campbell had no choice but to surrender. Galvez had conquered British West Florida. In the world-wide war Britain had suffered yet another defeat. When the time came for Spain and Britain to negotiate peace terms, both East and West Florida would become Spanish territory.

FORCES OF GENERAL BERNARDO DE GALVEZ

WEST FLORIDA FALLS TO SPAIN
Operating from New Orleans and Havana, Spanish land and naval forces cleared the West Florida coastline of British military posts.

SPANISH MUSKET
This type of infantry musket was used in the West Florida campaigns. They were also supplied to George Rogers Clark's Patriot force by Governor Galvez.

1757 MUSKET

ASSAULT ON PENSACOLA
After two months of siege, the Spanish finally break through British defenses at Pensacola. Soldiers carry scaling ladders to get over the walls.

Losses	
Spanish:	negligible
British:	105 killed, 1,169 wounded/prisoners

GREENE FIGHTS ON

Cornwallis wanted revenge after the Patriot victory at The Cowpens. Burning wagons and supplies that slowed his men down, he chased Morgan through North Carolina. The British were fast, but Morgan was faster. He joined forces with Greene's main army, and by February the rebels had escaped to Virginia.

Greene soon returned southward, hoping to lure the British into attacking him. The aggressive Cornwallis pounced on this chance to destroy Greene's army. Though outnumbered, Cornwallis believed his 1,900 veterans could beat any number of rebels.

At Guilford Court House, North Carolina, Greene arranged his mostly militia army of 4,300 into three defensive lines.

Painted drum made of wood, sheepskin, and linen

DRUM CARRIED AT
GUILFORD
COURT HOUSE

In the first two lines were the Carolina and Virginia militias. Behind them were Maryland and Delaware Continentals, the best fighters of the army. Greene knew the volunteer militia could not stand long against crack British troops. He counted on the Continentals to take whatever Cornwallis would throw at him.

On the morning of March 15, Cornwallis attacked. His weary Regulars had been marching hard without food for 12 hours, but they did not hesitate. The Patriot militias fought bravely before crumbling. The British

IN LINE OF BATTLE
Patriot "line troops," or infantry, prepare to meet the brunt of Cornwallis's assault. Colonel William Washington's dragoons, at rear, gallop forward to counterattack an enemy threat and prevent a breakthrough.

Losses		
American:	78 killed,	183 wounded
British:	143 killed,	389 wounded

next hit the Continentals, who stood up under the attack. Cornwallis's finest troops were savagely driven back. He rallied them and charged once again, but Greene now withdrew in a fighting retreat.

Cornwallis had won the battle, but lost too many veteran soldiers. The performance of his men at Guilford Court House is ranked with the best in British history. Yet, he did not win decisively. This was frustrating for Cornwallis, who withdrew to the North Carolina coast. Greene remained to fight another day. He had damaged Cornwallis, skillfully wearing down this dangerous opponent. Since arriving in America in 1776, Cornwallis had never been defeated in battle.

A CHASE TO VIRGINIA
Morgan retreated to North Carolina after the Battle of The Cowpens. Cornwallis followed fast from Winnsborough. Greene joined forces with Morgan and they escaped into Virginia. After being reinforced, Greene returned to North Carolina. Cornwallis attacked him at Guilford Court House.

▬▬▬ CORNWALLIS
▬▬▬ GREENE

THE LEADERSHIP

GREENE'S VETERAN GENERALS INCLUDED Maryland's Otho Williams and South Carolina's Isaac Huger. Cornwallis had top generals in Charles O'Hara and Alexander Leslie. O'Hara lost his son, an artillery lieutenant, in the battle.

CHARLES O'HARA (C. 1740-1802)
General O'Hara, of the famed Coldstream Guards, had served in Europe and Africa. He was a key commander in Cornwallis's southern campaign. O'Hara was wounded leading the attack that won the day at Guilford Court House.

"Another such victory would destroy the British army."
—Parliament's Charles Fox, on Guilford Court House

NATHANAEL GREENE (1742-1786)
A Rhode Islander with little previous military experience, Greene became Washington's most trusted officer. He once even accepted the thankless task of supplying the army. Greene's skillful generalship forced Cornwallis to Yorktown for reinforcements. This brought on the final showdown.

"I am determined to carry the war into South Carolina."
—Greene to Washington, after Guilford Court House

BATTLE IN THE SWAMPS

In March, Cornwallis went north to Virginia. Greene did not follow, but moved to break British control of South Carolina. Greene joined with guerrilla fighters Francis Marion and Thomas Sumter to capture key forts.

Lord Francis Rawdon commanded the British in South Carolina. That April, he beat Greene in a hard-fought battle at Hobkirk's Hill. Greene saved most of his army with a fighting retreat. He immediately began rebuilding his force until he had 2,400 troops.

Both armies suffered from the heat of the South Carolina summer. Lord Rawdon became so ill that he gave up command of his 2,000 men to Colonel Alexander Stewart. In September, Greene made a surprise attack on Stewart, who was camped at a swampy area named Eutaw Springs. After heavy fighting, Greene's troops drove the British out of their camp. Many of the tired and hungry Patriots stopped to loot enemy tents and supplies.

A group of Regulars under Major John Marjoribanks did not retreat, but stood firm against repeated American charges. Stewart rallied the rest of his men and counterattacked. Marjoribanks was killed, but the Patriots were forced to retreat. Though Stewart held the field, he lost far more men than Greene. The crippled British withdrew to Charleston.

Greene lost the battle, but won the campaign. South of Virginia, only the cities of Charleston and Savannah were

Losses	
American:	139 killed, 375 wounded, 8 prisoners/missing
British:	85 killed, 351 wounded, 430 prisoners/missing

VICTORY SEEMS NEAR
American troops under Nathanael Greene came close to victory at Eutaw Springs, South Carolina. Greene withdrew, but the British suffered heavily. It was the Revolution's last major battle before the Yorktown campaign.

still in British hands. Cornwallis was at Yorktown, Virginia. Before resuming the offensive, he waited for commander-in-chief Sir Henry Clinton to send supplies from New York City.

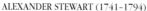

RAWDON AND STEWART   GREENE

EVEN FIGHT IN SOUTH CAROLINA
Greene maneuvered to bring on a battle with the outnumbered Stewart. The British held the field but withdrew toward Charleston. Both sides claimed victory.

REGIMENTAL DRAGON
The dragon on this shoulder belt plate was the symbol of the British 3rd Regiment, "The Buffs," who fought at Eutaw Springs.

THE LEADERSHIP

THE BEST SOUTHERN OFFICERS were with Greene: Henry Lee, Andrew Pickens, Francis Marion, Jethro Sumner, and William Washington. Stewart had Loyalist colonel John Cruger, former mayor of New York.

"[I] was at a loss which most to admire, the gallantry of the officers or the good conduct of the men."

—Greene, early in the battle

HENRY LEE (1756–1818)
Nicknamed "Light-Horse Harry," Colonel Lee led "Lee's Legion" of cavalry and infantry. Congress honored him for valor. A Virginian and a Princeton graduate, Lee was the father of Civil War Confederate general Robert E. Lee.

ALEXANDER STEWART (1741–1794)
Colonel Stewart brought his 3rd Regiment of Foot to Charleston in mid-1781. After taking over Rawdon's force at Eutaw Springs, Stewart returned to Charleston. There he commanded defensive works until the British evacuated the city.

"[T]hey rendered it impossible [to get information] by waylaying the by-paths and passes through the different swamps."

—Stewart reports on the Rebel scouts

SEA POWER TRAPS CORNWALLIS

Washington's army was camped north of British-held New York City in the summer of 1781. Since losing the city in 1776, Washington had sworn to one day recapture it. Clinton had 10,000 troops there.

Together with French general Rochambeau's 4,000 soldiers in Newport, Rhode Island, Washington hoped to attack Clinton. To do this the Allies asked for the help of the French fleet in the West Indies, commanded by Admiral De Grasse.

In August, De Grasse sent word that he was not sailing to New York, but was going to Chesapeake Bay instead. There, he could block Cornwallis's escape by sea if Washington and Rochambeau marched south to besiege Yorktown. De Grasse also had an additional 3,000 troops. Rochambeau and Washington agreed

with this plan. Washington knew he had to move fast to trap Cornwallis. Congress, however, had no money to pay the Patriot troops or finance the march south. Rochambeau came to the rescue, offering Washington half the money in his own army's war chest. The Allies began to move.

At first, they pretended to be preparing an attack on New York. This held Clinton's forces in position there. By the time Clinton realized his enemies were going after Cornwallis, the Patriots and French were parading through Philadelphia. The Allies journeyed rapidly toward Yorktown as Clinton organized reinforcements for Cornwallis. These would be carried by the British Navy to Yorktown if De

BATTLE OF THE VIRGINIA CAPES
Cannons roar and sails billow as British warships, right, attack the French fleet. French Admiral de Grasse drove British admirals Graves and Hood away from Chesapeake Bay. Cornwallis was blockaded at Yorktown.

Losses	
French:	220 killed/wounded
British:	90 killed, 246 wounded

Grasse's warships did not stop them.

On September 14, Washington arrived near Yorktown. He soon heard welcome news that De Grasse had outfought the British off the Virginia capes. British admirals Thomas Graves and Samuel Hood sailed back to New York in defeat. The Chesapeake was blockaded, and Cornwallis could not escape. The Allies must force his surrender before an even stronger British fleet appeared.

RIVAL FLEETS RACE TO THE CHESAPEAKE
French fleets sailed to Yorktown from Newport, Rhode Island and the West Indies. The British came from New York to rescue Cornwallis, but De Grasse got there first. To save Cornwallis's army, the British had no choice but to attack the French fleet.

THE LEADERSHIP

Hood and Graves, with 19 ships, were outnumbered by De Grasse's 24 ships. The French soon were reinforced by the arrival of Admiral de Barras's 12 warships.

"[I don't know] what to say in the truly lamentable state we have brought ourselves."

—Hood answers Graves's request for advice

SAMUEL HOOD (1724-1816)
Admiral Hood came out of retirement for the American war. Second in command to Graves, Hood complained that his commander was "unequal to the conducting of a great squadron." Hood helped defeat De Grasse the following spring.

"[We saw] by the sailing of the English that they had suffered greatly."

—A French naval officer, after the engagement

FRANCOIS JOSEPH COMTE DE GRASSE (1722-1788)
Admiral De Grasse served in the navy from the age of 11. He rose in rank because of his military success. By arriving at Yorktown before Graves and Hood, De Grasse won the advantage, forcing them to attack him. Just after Yorktown, he was defeated and captured by the British.

THE ALLIES TRIUMPHANT

The approximately 8,300 British and Germans with Cornwallis at Yorktown were trapped inside their earthwork defenses. Camped all around were more than 17,000 Americans and French under Washington and Rochambeau. The Americans accounted for about 8,900 of the Allies' force, with 5,700 of them Continentals.

Blocking escape and resupply by sea was Admiral De Grasse's fleet. Another French squadron under Admiral Barras had arrived from Newport, Rhode Island, bringing heavy siege cannon to bombard the Yorktown defenses.

Although Cornwallis had some of the finest British troops in America, he was too outnumbered to counterattack. All he could do was hope that Clinton would send reinforcements to save him. Cornwallis was told to expect the fleet in mid-October. With the French Navy dominating the sea lanes to Yorktown, however, the British were unable to get through.

There were a few small attacks and counterattacks at Yorktown, and the Allies gained ground. As the days went by, the Americans and French dug their

THE LEADERSHIP

MANY OF WASHINGTON'S TOP GENERALS were at Yorktown: Lincoln, Knox, Von Steuben, Lafayette, Wayne, Muhlenberg, Moses Hazen, and New York's James Clinton. Cornwallis had only one general, Charles O'Hara.

JEAN-BAPTISTE COMTE DE ROCHAMBEAU (1725–1807)
A highly respected officer, Rochambeau arrived in America in mid-1780 to head the French army. Until then, the French had little success in the war. Rochambeau fully supported Washington's strategy at Yorktown and gave him credit for the victory.

"You are mistaken, the commander-in-chief of our army is on the right."

—A French officer, directing O'Hara toward Washington

CHARLES CORNWALLIS (1738–1805)
Lord Cornwallis remained highly regarded in Britain after Yorktown. He served terms as governor-general of India and Ireland. Cornwallis won several important battles as governor, and was also an excellent administrator.

"I have the mortification to inform your Excellency that I have been forced…to surrender… to the combined forces of America and France."

—Cornwallis, in a report to Clinton

trenches ever closer to the British positions. Soon, heavy guns were firing right into Yorktown, smashing buildings and starting fires.

Then, on the night of October 15, a few hundred Americans and French made daring bayonet attacks. They captured two redoubts that were key to the British defenses. Cannon taken in the redoubts were turned on the British the next day. In the face of such destructive point-blank fire, Cornwallis had to surrender.

On October 19, the British army marched out to surrender. Yorktown was Washington's greatest victory and the last major battle of the Revolution.

WASHINGTON AND THE FRENCH

Artillery bombards Yorktown and allied troops capture enemy positions as the generals discuss strategy. The flags of the United States and France fly above the headquarters tent, where Washington studies a map and Rochambeau addresses an officer.

AMERICAN AND FRENCH

MARCH TO YORKTOWN

Washington was overall allied commander for this campaign. In a month-long journey, his American and French troops traveled more than 350 miles (363 kilometers) to Yorktown.

Fuse hole

MORTAR SHELL

Iron mortar shells were filled with gunpowder, their fuses lit, and they were fired from a cannon. When the fuse burned down, the shell exploded. This 13-inch (33-centimeter) French shell was found near Yorktown.

Losses

American/French: 83 killed, 158 wounded
British/German: 156 killed, 326 wounded, 7,310 prisoners/missing

An Uneasy Truce, a Welcome Peace

Washington laid siege to the enemy garrison in New York City, and Greene watched British-held Charleston and Savannah. There were no more battles, but small skirmishes cost lives on both sides.

In mid-1782, peace negotiations began in Paris. That November, preliminary terms were signed, and hostilities stopped. The British withdrew from Wilmington, North Carolina, and from Savannah and Charleston. Only New York remained under their control. Washington remained with his army while the months dragged slowly by. As America's great war hero, he could have gone home to Mount Vernon and given someone else the thankless task of continuing the siege. Instead, he kept his promise to stay until the last British soldier left New York City.

With peace at hand, Congress neglected its army. Officers were furious because they had not been

THE GENERAL RESIGNS
George Washington offers his resignation to members of Congress at Annapolis, Maryland, on December 23, 1783. When the ceremony was over, he mounted his waiting horse and rode home to Mount Vernon.

HUDSON RIVER HEADQUARTERS
After Yorktown, Washington spent much of his time living in this Newburgh, New York, farmhouse. Positioned to overlook the Hudson just above West Point, these quarters were near his army's base at New Windsor.

March 1782	April 1782	June 1782	November 1782
British Prime Minister Lord North resigns and a new government takes power	Sir Guy Carleton becomes commander of British forces in America. Washington headquartered at Newburgh, New York	British evacuate Savannah, Georgia	Preliminary peace treaty is signed between Britain and the United States

paid for years, and many were in debt. In the spring of 1783, they threatened to mutiny and march on Congress. Washington stood before them and warned of the dangers if the military overthrew Congress. He convinced them not to mutiny after all they had done for their country.

Soon, the Continental Army was disbanded regiment by regiment, and the men went home, yet to be paid.

The "Peace of Paris" was signed on September 3, 1783, and the British evacuated New York City in late November. Washington celebrated there for a few days, then went to Congress and resigned as commander-in-chief.

MAKING PEACE

America's peace negotiations with Great Britain were complicated and slow-moving. France wanted some control over the peace terms. France and Spain opposed American claims to the Mississippi region. By fall of 1783, a peace was made with Britain, which recognized American independence. Unresolved issues with other nations were set aside. Benjamin Franklin wrote, "There never was a good war or a bad peace."

PEACE OF PARIS

Official wax seals

AMERICAN COMMISSIONERS
l-r: John Jay, John Adams, Franklin, Henry Laurens, and Franklin's secretary and nephew William Temple Franklin.

December 1782	September 1783	November 1798	December 1783
British evacuate Charleston, South Carolina and most of the troops sail to New York City	The Peace of Paris is signed by the United States, Great Britain, France, Spain, and the Netherlands	Washington enters New York City as the British leave	Washington resigns from command of the Continental Army

A TWILIGHT WAR

After Yorktown, many Americans thought the war was over, but Washington warned against overconfidence. The British might open a new campaign, especially if they got the better of the French. Americans must remain alert, because a surprise enemy attack could destroy all the Revolution had won.

New York City was strongly defended by the troops of Sir Guy Carleton, who replaced Clinton in May. Carleton had held Canada against the rebel invasions. Washington's army was based at New Windsor, New York, north of the city. His men were kept ready for any British move, but they were sick of war and unhappy at not being paid. The main British forces in the South were at Charleston and Savannah, under the command of General Alexander Leslie.

Sharp skirmishing continued here and there as bitter Loyalists refused to give up the struggle. Most had lost all they owned because of the war. They had no idea what would happen to them in the future. Some were going to Britain, others to new settlements in Canada. Loyalist fighters in the South raided Patriot positions and fought with Greene's forces.

In August, Colonel John Laurens was killed in one of these clashes. Once an important headquarters aide to Washington, Laurens died just outside Charleston, his hometown. He was the son of Henry Laurens, a South Carolina congressional delegate and now a peace commissioner in Paris. A former president of Congress, Henry Laurens was one of Washington's strongest allies. Washington was heartbroken at the loss of John

EVACUATION OF CHARLESTON
British troops and Loyalists row to ships, leaving Charleston on December 14, 1782. The South was now free of the king's forces. The only major British garrison in the former colonies was at New York City.

Losses: Southern Engagements	
American:	43 killed, 129 wounded, 211 prisoners/missing
British:	64 killed, 91 wounded

Laurens, one of the last casualties of the Revolution.

That winter, Carleton ordered Leslie to transport the southern garrisons to New York, and the South was free. Still, no final treaty had yet been signed to officially end the war.

WITHDRAWAL TO NEW YORK
The British garrisons of Wilmington, North Carolina, and Savannah were shipped to Charleston in mid-1782. That winter they went to New York, which was evacuated a year later. ▬▬ BRITISH FORCES

THE LEADERSHIP

GREENE MAINTAINED AN ARMY in the South until August 1783, when he returned home. Washington stayed with the northern army until the British left New York City on November 25, 1783. Clinton had been replaced at New York by Guy Carleton in May 1782.

ALEXANDER LESLIE (1740-1794)
General Leslie was stationed in Canada at the start of the war. He went on to serve at Boston, New York, New Jersey, and in the South. Leslie was a courageous officer who personally led his men into battle. He replaced Cornwallis as commander in the South after Yorktown.

"It was a war in which...we had suffered everything without gaining anything.... Every point of the war was against us."

—Member of Parliament, calling for an end to hostilities

"[W]ith our fate will the destiny of millions be involved."

—George Washington, in an open letter to America in 1783

JOHN LAURENS (1754-1782)
Colonel Laurens was an aide to Washington and saw action in many major battles. He was wounded twice and captured once. Fluent in French, he went to France in 1781 to help arrange a loan. He returned in time to fight at Yorktown, where he negotiated Cornwallis's surrender.

THE FINAL TRIUMPH

Most states were peaceful after Yorktown, and they disbanded their troops. New York City remained under siege during 1783. As Washington and Carleton waited for the peace treaty to be signed, they arranged for a smooth takeover of the city. There would be no looting or attacks on Loyalists.

On November 25, the last Regulars rowed out to the waiting British fleet, and Washington rode into New York. He led a small group of officers and civilians, including Governor George Clinton. Only a few hundred

"GB" Georgia Battalion

soldiers marched along, because the rest of the army had been discharged. The victory parade was modest, with little military pomp. New York was run down and shabby after seven years of military occupation.

There followed some days of banquets, speechmaking, and fireworks. Then Washington called his remaining officers to Fraunces Tavern on December 4.

To get as many officers as possible to the occasion, several young artillerymen were invited.

PEWTER BUTTON
This button is from the Georgia Battalion, formed early in 1783. The unit was disbanded later that year.

ENTERING NEW YORK CITY
Washington leads Patriot officers and dignitaries into Manhattan just hours after the last British troops departed. New York had been a fortress city under British and Loyalist control since 1776.

Revolutionary War Army Deaths	
American:	approximately 4,500
British/German:	approximately 2,000
French:	approximately 400
Spanish:	approximately 100

Still, the group numbered fewer than 40. Washington wished them well and asked each one to come and shake his hand. Many were in tears as their general bade them a final farewell.

The next day, Washington set out on horseback for Annapolis, Maryland, where Congress was sitting. All along the way were cheering crowds and celebrations. At Annapolis, on December 23, George Washington resigned as Commander-in-Chief of the Armies of the United States of America.

■ BRITISH EVACUATION

SAILING AWAY
With the tide and a fair wind, the Royal Navy carried Carleton's garrison out of New York harbor and past Long Island into the Atlantic.

THE LEADERSHIP

THE GENERALS WITH WASHINGTON were Knox, James Clinton, Van Cortlandt, Von Steuben, and New Yorker Alexander McDougall. Carleton's commandant for the city was General James Robertson.

"With a heart full of love and gratitude, I now take leave of you."
—Washington, bidding farewell to his officers

GEORGE WASHINGTON (1732-1799)
General Washington longed to go back to Mount Vernon and retire, but he stayed with the army until New York City was free. He had made this promise when the city fell to Howe in mid-1776.

"At last, the fatal day has come."
—George III, recognizing defeat and considering abdication

KING GEORGE III (1738-1820)
The king was shattered by the loss of the American colonies. When his pro-war prime minister, Lord North, resigned in disgrace, King George considered giving up the throne. He changed his mind and ruled until his death in 1820.

FOES IN THE REVOLUTION

PATRIOTS AND FRENCH

JOHN ADAMS
Massachusetts congressional delegate; drafter of Declaration of Independence; peace commissioner.

BENJAMIN FRANKLIN
Pennsylvania congressional delegate; drafter of Declaration of Independence; minister to France; peace commissioner.

JOHN DICKINSON
Congressional delegate, worked for peaceful settlement with Britain; colonel of first Philadelphia battalion.

JOHN HANCOCK
Wealthy Massachusetts merchant; congressional delegate and president; first to sign the Declaration.

ALEXANDER HAMILTON
Born in the West Indies; New York artillery officer and Washington's headquarters aide; led key assault at Yorktown.

PATRICK HENRY
Virginia statesman and advocate of independence; governor of Virginia; authorized George Rogers Clark expedition.

THOMAS JEFFERSON
Virginia congressional delegate and drafter of the Declaration of Independence; Patriot governor of Virginia.

BARON JOHANN DE KALB
Bavarian volunteer, Patriot general; served in Southern Theater; killed at Battle of Camden in 1780.

HENRY LAURENS
South Carolina congressional delegate and president; captured by British; peace treaty commissioner.

"Our success must be attributed to the justice of our cause and the bravery of our troops." —General Daniel Morgan

BRITISH, LOYALISTS, HESSIANS

JOHN ANDRÉ
Major and deputy adjutant general for headquarters; negotiated with Arnold, caught and executed as a spy in 1780.

EDMUND BURKE
Statesman; opposed King's American policies; made powerful speeches in Parliament against the war.

JOHN MURRAY
Lord Dunmore was royal governor of Virginia; led Loyalist raids against Patriots; driven out in mid-1776.

GEORGE GERMAIN
British secretary of state for America; planned war strategy and was blamed for interfering with generals.

THOMAS HUTCHINSON
Pre-war royal governor of Massachusetts, opposed Patriot resistance in Boston; replaced by Gage in 1774.

JOHN JOHNSON
New York Loyalist, knighted for service in Indian conflicts; led raids in the Mohawk Valley; settled in Canada.

FREDERICK NORTH
Prime minister and a Tory, Lord North led his government's war effort; resigned after Yorktown.

RICHARD PEARSON
As captain of the 44-gun HMS *Serapis,* lost famous North Sea battle with John Paul Jones's *Bonhomme Richard* in 1779.

HUGH PERCY
A highly respected general, Lord Percy served in key early battles, but opposed the war; returned home in 1777.

PATRIOTS AND FRENCH

ANNE-CÉSAR DE LA LUZERNE
French duke and ambassador to U.S. after 1779; influential consultant to Congress.

FRANCIS MARION
South Carolina partisan, the "Swamp Fox"; led Patriot fighters in the South.

ROBERT MORRIS
Pennsylvania merchant, raised funds for the Patriots; the "Financier of the Revolution."

FRIEDRICH WILHELM VON STEUBEN
Prussian officer termed "the first teacher of the American army"; as inspector general of army, trained officers in drill methods.

COUNT DE VERGENNES
French foreign minister who persuaded his government to support the Revolution, first secretly, then with an alliance.

BRITISH, LOYALISTS, HESSIANS

WILLIAM PHILLIPS
Veteran general and artillerist captured with Burgoyne and later exchanged.

WILLIAM PITT
British opposition leader who opposed government policies in America.

BARRY ST. LEGER
Experienced in frontier warfare; his campaign to join Burgoyne was defeated in 1777.

FRIEDRICH ADOLPHUS VON RIEDESEL
German general, Burgoyne's second-in-command; his wife accompanied him and kept a colorful memoir of her experiences.

GEORGE RODNEY
Admiral serving in Atlantic and Caribbean; failed to prevent French fleet reaching American waters for the Yorktown campaign.

INDEX

A–D

Adams, John, 8, 87, 92
Agnew, James, 53
Albany, N.Y., 13, 45, 48
Alexander, William, 34–35
Allen, Ethan, 14
Andre, John, 61, 93
Arnold, Benedict, 10–11, 14, 24–26, 36, 45, 47–49, 61, 74–75,
Barras, Louis, Comte de, 83–84
Bennington, Vermont, 41, 45
Bonhomme Richard, 11, 60, 63, 93
Boone, Daniel, 41
Boonesboro, Kentucky, 41, 55
Boston, 6, 10, 12, 14–23, 25, 28–29, 89
Boston, Siege of, 10, 20–23
Brandywine, Battle of, 7, 10, 41, 50–51, 53
Brant, Joseph, 46–47
Breed's Hill, Battle of, 10, 14–15, 17–20
Bunker Hill, 18
Burgoyne, John, 10, 22, 36, 40–41, 44–50, 75,
Burke, Edmund, 93
Burke, Thomas, 51
Camden, Battle of, 11–12, 45, 61, 67–68
Campbell, John, 30–31, 76–77
Canada, Invasion of, 10, 12, 15, 24–27
Carleton, Guy Sir, 8, 11, 24–28, 86, 88–91
Caswell, Richard, 30–31
Charleston (1st), Siege of, 10–11, 28, 32–33
Charleston (2nd), Siege of, 66
Charleston, S.C., 6, 11–12, 28–33, 60–61, 65–66, 68, 71, 80–81, 86–88
Chesapeake Capes, Battle of, 11, 12–13, 71, 82–83
Chew, Benjamin, 52
Clark, George Rogers, 11, 54–55, 58–59, 77
Clinton, George, 90
Clinton, Henry, 11, 22, 31–35, 51, 54–57, 60, 62, 66, 82, 88–89
Clinton, James, 84, 91
Colbraith, William, 47
Combahee Ferry, S.C., 11
Concord, Mass., 2–3, 6, 10, 14, 16–17, 30
Cornwallis, Charles, 11–12, 31, 33, 35, 40, 42–43, 51, 57, 61, 67, 68–75, 79, 80, 82, 84, 89
Cowpens, Battle of, 11, 12, 70, 72–73, 79
Cruger, John, 81
Dale, Richard, 63
Dawes, William, 16
Dickinson, John, 92
Dorchester Heights, 22–23

E–G

Elphinstone, George, 66
Estaing, Count Charles d', 64–65

Eutaw Springs, Battle of, 11–12, 71, 80–81
Evacuation Day, 90–91
Ferguson, Patrick, 51, 68–69
Fleury, Teissedre de, 62
Fort Detroit, 55, 58–59
Fort Knyphausen, 37
Fort Lee, N.J., 10, 29, 37
Fort Michilimackinac, 55
Fort Sackville, 54, 58
Fort Stanwix, N.Y. 46–47
Fort Ticonderoga, 10, 14, 20, 27, 36, 40, 44
Fort Washington, N.Y. 10, 29, 37
Franklin, Benjamin, 8, 10, 35, 51, 55, 87, 92
Franklin, William Temple, 87
Fraser, Simon, 44–45, 48–49
Freeman's Farm, N.Y. 48–49
French and Indian War, 6, 8, 17–18, 21–22, 26, 31, 43, 48–49, 59
Gage, Thomas, 6, 8, 14–15, 18–21, 30–31
Galvez, Bernardo de, 76–77
Gansevoort, Peter, 46–47
Gates, Horatio, 8, 11, 27, 41, 45, 48, 61, 67, 69,
George III, King, 6–8, 10, 15, 22, 30, 35, 44, 91
Germain, George, 93
Germantown, Battle of, 10, 40–41, 52–53
Gibault, Père, 59
Gist, Mordecai, 67
Glover, John, 38, 48
Grasse, Francois Joseph, Comte De, 82–84
Graves, Thomas, 82–83
Green Spring, Virginia, 75
Greene, Nathanael, 11, 37, 52, 54, 61, 69, 70–72, 78–81, 86, 89
Guilford Court House, Battle of, 11–12, 70, 78–79

H–K

Hale, Nathan, 10
Hamilton, Alexander, 43, 67, 92
Hamilton, Henry, 58–59
Hancock, John, 8–10, 92
Harlem Heights, Battle of, 10, 29, 35
Hazen, Moses, 84
Heister, Philip von, 35
Henry, Patrick, 92
Herkimer, Nicholas, 46–47
Hobkirk's Hill, Battle of, 70, 80
Hogun, James, 66
Hood, Samuel, 82–83
Howe, Richard, 35
Howe, William, 10–11, 18–20, 22, 28, 34–35, 37–38, 40–41, 44–45, 48, 50–54, 57, 91
Hubbardton, Battle of, 10, 40
Huger, Isaac, 79
Hutchinson, Thomas, 93

J–M

Jay, John, 87
Jefferson, Thomas, 8, 29, 92
Johnson, Henry, 62

Johnson, John, 93
Jones, John Paul, 60, 63
Kalb, Baron Johann De, 67, 92
Kaskaskia, 55, 58
King's Mountain, Battle of, 11, 61, 68–69
Knox, Henry, 10, 20–22, 39, 84, 91
Knyphausen, Baron Wilhelm von, 35, 37, 51
Lafayette, Marie Joseph du Motier, Marquis de, 51, 70, 74–75, 84
Lafayette's Virginia Campaign, 70, 74–75
Laurens, Henry, 87–88, 92
Laurens, John, 88–89
Lee, Charles, 33, 56–57
Lee, Henry, 81
Leslie, Alexander, 79, 88–89
Lexington and Concord, Battle of, 6, 10, 14–17, 30
Lincoln, Benjamin, 11, 48, 64–66, 71, 84
Livingston, Robert, 8
Long Island, Battle of, 10, 28, 34–35
Long Knives' Campaign, 58–59
Louis XVI, King, 55
Luzerne, Anne–Cesar de la, 94
Maclean, Allan, 26
Magaw, Robert, 37
Mahwood, Charles, 43
Marion, Francis, 80–81, 94
Marjoribanks, John, 80
Martin, Josiah, 30–31
McDonald, Donald, 30–31
McDougall, Alexander, 91
McLeod, Donald, 30–31
Mercer, Hugh, 42–43
Monckton, Henry, 57
Monmouth Courthouse, 55
Monmouth, Battle of, 11, 54, 56–57
Montgomery, Richard, 8, 10, 24–26,
Montreal, 15, 24–25, 27–28
Moore, James, 30–31
Moore's Creek Bridge, Battle of, 10, 28, 30–31
Morgan, Daniel, 26–27, 41, 45, 70, 72–73, 78–79
Morris, Robert, 94
Morristown, N.J., 10–11, 40, 43, 60
Moultrie, William, 32–33, 66
Muhlenberg, Peter, 53, 84
Murphy, Timothy, 49
Murray, John, 93
Musgrave, Thomas, 52–53

N–Q

Napoleonic Wars, 35
New Orleans, 76–77
New Windsor, N.Y., 86, 88
New York City, 6, 23, 28, 34, 37, 44, 47, 57, 71, 82, 86– 90
Newburgh, N.J., 11, 86
Newport, R.I., 11, 55, 61, 82, 84
North, Lord Frederick, 11, 86, 91, 93

O'Hara, Charles, 79, 84
Oriskany, Battle of, 10, 40, 46–47
Paine, Thomas, 10, 38
Parker, John, 16–17
Parker, Peter, 32–33
Pearson, Richard, 63, 93
Pensacola, Siege of, 76
Pensacola, West Florida, 11, 76–77
Percy, Hugh, 93
Philadelphia, 6, 8, 10–12, 14–15, 29, 41, 45, 50–54, 56, 82
Phillips, William, 75, 94
Pickens, Andrew, 81
Pickering, Timothy, 53
Pitcairn, John, 17
Pitt, William, 94
Poor, Enoch, 48
Prevost, Augustine, 64–65
Princeton, Battle of, 10, 40, 42–43
Pulaski, Casimir, 65
Putnam, Israel, 8, 18–19
Quebec, Invasion of, 10, 12, 15, 24–27

R–T

Rall, Johann von, 37–39
Rawdon, Francis, 67, 80
Revere, Paul 14, 16
Riedesel, Friedrich Adolphus von, 44–45, 94
Robertson, James, 91

Rochambeau, Jean-Baptiste, Comte de, 11, 61, 71, 82, 84–85
Rodney, George, 94
Rogers, Robert, 8
Rutledge, John, 33
Saint Johns, Canada 15, 24, 27
St. Leger, Barry, 44, 46–48, 94
Saratoga Campaign, 40-41, 44–49
Saratoga, Battles of, 10, 41, 48–49
Savannah, Georgia, 6, 11–12, 55, 60, 64–66, 71, 81, 86, 88–89
Savannah, Siege of, 11, 60, 64–65
Schuyler, Philip, 24, 36, 44
Serapis, HMS, 11, 60, 63, 93
Seven Years' War, 6, 55
Shelby, Isaac, 68
Sherman, Roger, 8
Simcoe, John Graves, 74–75
Smallwood, William, 67
Smith, Francis, 17
Stark, John, 8, 45, 49
Steuben, Baron Friedrich Wilhelm von, 11, 53, 54, 62, 75, 84, 91, 94
Stewart, Alexander, 80–81
Stirling, Lord, 34–35
Stony Point, Battle of, 11, 60, 62
Sullivan, John, 26–27, 51–52
Sumner, Jethro, 81
Sumter, Thomas, 80
Tarleton, Banastre, 66, 72–73

Thayendanega, 46–47
Thomas, John, 26
Trenton, Battle of, 10, 29, 38–39

V–Z

Valcour Island, Battle of, 10, 28–29, 36–37
Valley Forge, Penn., 10, 41, 53–54
Van Cortlandt, Philip, 45, 91
Vergennes, Count de, 94
Vincennes, 55, 58
Virginia Capes, Battle of, 11, 12–13, 71, 82–83
Virginia Campaign, Lafayette's, 70, 74–75
Warren, Joseph, 16
Washington, George, 1, 4, 8, 10, 12, 14–15, 20–23, 28–29, 34–35, 37–43, 45, 50, 52–53, 55, 57, 60, 69–71, 82–83, 85–87, 89–91
Washington, William, 72–73
Wayne, Anthony, 62, 71, 75, 84
West Point, N.Y., 61–62, 86
White Plains, Battle of, 10, 29
Willett, Marinus, 47
Williams, Otho, 79
Woodford, William, 66
Wyoming Valley, Penn., 11, 54
Yorktown Campaign, 11–12, 70–71, 80, 82–85
Yorktown, Virginia, 11–13, 70–71, 75, 80–86, 88–90

ACKNOWLEDGMENTS
Media Projects, Inc. and DK Publishing, Inc. offer their grateful thanks to: artist and collector Don Troiani, Historical Art Prints, www.historicalartprints.com; René Chartrand, of Canada's National Historic Sites; Peter Harrington of the Anne S. K. Brown Military Collection, Brown University Library; Catherine H. Grosfils, Colonial Williamsburg Foundation; Andrea Ashby, Independence National Historical Park; Christopher D. Fox, Fort Ticonderoga Museum; Richard Malley, Connecticut Historical Society; and Rob Stokes and James Burmester for cartography.

Photography and Art Credits
(t=top; b=bottom; l=left; r=right; c=center; a=above)
The American Revolution, by John Fiske: 10l, 19br, 22br, 35cl, 35br, 36cl, 37cl, 38bl, 39b, 43cl, 47cl, 48cl, 51br, 57cl, 57br, 67cl, 68cl, 83br, 84br, 89br, 92cr, 93tl, 93tc, 93cl, 93c, 93cr, 93bl, 93bc, 93br, 94tl, 94tc, 94acr, 94cl, 94cb, 94rc, 94bl, 94br. Anne S. K. Brown Military Collection, Brown University Library: 2–3c, 16b, 19cl, 22c, 27b, 63br, 66br, 67br. Architect of the Capitol: 8–9b, 32b, 40–41b, 70–71b, 79cl, 86tr. The Bridgeman Art Library: 7t Private Collection; 7c American Illustrators Gallery, NYC; 21c Yale Center for British Art; 24br New-York Historical Society; 28–29b Delaware Art Museum; 29cr Delaware Art Museum, Wilmington; 43br Private Collection; 45cl New-York Historical Society; 47br National Gallery of Canada; 52b Delaware Art Museum, Wilmington; 60–61b Delaware Art Museum, Wilmington; 62br Library of Congress; 64br Chateau de Versailles, France; 71cr Delaware Art Museum, Wilmington; 73br National Gallery, London; 74b New-York Historical Society; 83cl National Maritime Museum, London; 84cl Chateau de Versailles, France; 85b Chateau de Versailles, France; 88b Delaware Art Museum, Wilmington; 91br The Crown Estate. Brooklyn Historical Society: 34b. James Burmester: 5br, 15t. Canadian Archives: 75br. Courtesy of René Chartrand: 24cl. Clements Library, University of Michigan: 89cl. Courtesy Colonel Charles Waterhouse Historical Museum: 36b. Colonial Williamsburg Foundation: 6t. The Connecticut

Historical Society Hartford, Connecticut: 23c. Delaware Art Museum: 14–15b. Duart Castle, courtesy of Sir Lachlan Maclean: 26tl. Courtesy of His Grace the Duke of Argyll: 76bl. Fort Ticonderoga Museum: 20b. Gibbs Museum of Art/Carolina Art Association: 33cl. Guilford Courthouse National Park: 78c. Independence National Historical Park: 9t, 21br, 26cr, 29tr, 45br, 53cl, 62cl, 63cl, 66cl, 73cl, 75cl, 79br, 81cl, 91cl, 92tl, 92tr, 92cl, 92c, 92bl, 92bc, 92br, 94tr, 94acl. Kentucky Historical Society: 41tc. Library of Congress: 8t, 11l, 11r, 13cr, 15c, 28cl, 38cr, 40tr, 41cr, 42b, 48br, 51cl, 54–55b, 55cr, 59cl, 60cr, 61cr, 65b, 69b, 70cr, 86–87b, 90b, 92tc. Photo from the collection of the Lexington, Massachusetts Historical Society: 17br. Moore's Creek National Battlefield: 30bl (Gill Cohen), 31cl, 31br. National Archives: 14t, 54cl, 58b, 87c. Courtesy of the National Museum of the U.S. Army (Charles McBarron): 49b, 56b, 59br, 78b. National Park Service/©Louis S. Glanzman: 23b. Courtesy of the National Park Service, Kings Mountain National Military Park: 68br. Courtesy of the Pensacola Historical Society: 76cr, 77b. Private Collection: 25b. Savannah Historical Society: 64cl. Photograph Courtesy of Sotheby's, Inc. © 2003: 81br. From the Collections of the SC Historical Society: 33br, 80b. Paintings by Don Troiani, www.historicalartprints.com: 12c, 17c, 18b, 44b, 50b, 72b. Courtesy of Don Troiani, www.historicalartprints.com: 4t, 4b, 5t, 5cl, 5cr, 17t, 18t, 25c, 26b, 30c, 33tc, 34c, 36cr, 39c, 42cr, 44c, 47t, 49cr, 51tl, 52c, 53br, 57tr, 59t, 63c, 64tc, 66bc, 69 cr, 71tr, 73tl, 74cr, 77c, 81tl, 85cr, 90c. U.S. Naval Academy: 37b. Naval Historical Center, U.S. Navy: 13br, 82b. Used with permission of the Utica (NY) Public Library: 10r, 46b. Commonwealth of Virginia: 93tr. Copyright 1996, Virginia Historical Society: 1c. Courtesy, Winterthur Museum: 87cr.

Cover Credits:
James Burmester: back flap t. Colonial Williamsburg Foundation: front br. Library of Congress: front bl, back flap b. National Museum of American History: front flap. Paintings by Don Troiani, www.historicalartprints.com: front tr, back c. Smithsonian American Art Museum: front tc. U.S. Senate: front tl.